HAMLET
Sports Special

Rugby

HAMLET
Sports Special

Rugby

Hamlyn
London · New York · Sydney · Toronto

The photographs on the cover and preliminary pages are:
Front cover Ireland playing Scotland in the Five Nations Championship in 1982. Ireland won the championship after being last the season before.
Back cover England playing Wales in 1982. Peter Winterbottom of England challenging Terry Holmes and Alun Donovan.
Title spread Wales playing France in the 1982 championship. The Welsh No 8 Jeff Squire powering his way through the French defence.

This book was commissioned by 'Hamlet' Cigars

'Hamlet' and 'Benson and Hedges' are registered trade marks in the United Kingdom of J. R. Freeman & Son Limited and Benson & Hedges Limited respectively: both companies are subsidiaries of Gallaher Limited.

Acknowledgements

The pictures in this book were obtained from the following sources:

Mike Brett Photography: 70 (top), 70 (below), 71 (below), 73 (top), 73 (below), 74, 75, 77 (top), 77 (below), 78, 79, 81, 82, 83 (top), 83 (below), 84 (top), 84 (below), 85 (top), 85 (below), 86, 87, 93 (top), 93 (below); Central Press Photos: 17, 41 (below), 49 (top), 49 (centre), 49 (below), 50 (top), 59 (below), 60 (top), 60 (below), 65 (top), 65 (below); Colorsport: front cover, 14 (top), 14 (below), 15, 16, 18 (top), 18 (below), 19, 20, 23, 25 (top), 26 (top), 26-27, 31, (right), 34 (below), 38 (below), 39, 40, 41 (top), 41 (centre), 42, 44, 45, 51, 52 (below), 54, 55 (below), 57, 58 (top), 58 (below), 59 (top), 61 (top), 61 (below), 62, 63 (top), 63 (below), 89 (top), 89 (below), 90, 91 (below); Mary Evans Picture Library: 8 (below), 37 (top); Hamlyn Group Picture Library: 8 (left); Irish Times: 24; Mansell Collection: 7, 9, 10, 10-11, 11 (top), 12 (top), 12 (below), 33, 36 (top), 48, 53, Press Association London: 31 (left); Sport & General Press Agency: 21 (top), 22, 25 (below), 26 (below), 32, 36 (below), 37 (below), 50 (centre), 50 (below), 52 (top), 52 (centre), 55 (top), 55 (centre), 56; Sporting Pictures (UK) Ltd: 66 (top), 66 (below), 71 (top), 91 (top), 92, 94, 94-95, 95; Bob Thomas Sports Photography, Northampton: title page, 27 (top), 27 (below), 30, 34 (top), 35, 38 (top), 43, 46 (top), 46 (below), back cover; Western Mail & Echo, Cardiff: 21 (below).

Published 1982 by
The Hamlyn Publishing Group Limited
London · New York · Sydney · Toronto
Astronaut House, Feltham, Middlesex, England

ISBN 0 600 34647 1

Printed in Italy

Contents

Introduction 6
Benny Green

The Evolution of Rugby 8
Stephen Jones

Famous Rugby Union Clubs 13
Stephen Jones

Great Union Players 19
David Norrie

The Five Nations Championship 33
Mervyn Davies

The Overseas Sides 47
David Norrie

The Origins of the League 64
David Howes

The Rugby League Clubs 67
David Howes

Great Rugby League Players 80
David Howes

Rugby Now 88
Stephen Jones and David Howes

Introduction

Benny Green

Through a chapter of accidents which has no place in the annals of Rugby Union, in 1941 I found myself on the threshold of my teens attending the William Ellis School at Parliament Hill Fields in north London. It was a relief to reach there, for apart from being located in my home town, as distinct from my parent school, St. Marylebone Grammar, which was buried somewhere in Cornwall, the William Ellis School, masquerading under its wartime designation of the North London Emergency, played soccer, whereas my parent school preferred rugby. And therein resided the greatest of ironies, because although never in my life have I known any community more passionately dedicated to the proposition that football is the only true satisfactory religion as that community perched up on Parliament Hill, we were still dimly aware that this William Ellis after whom our little home-from-home had been named, had once committed so blatantly the offence of hand-ball that from his misdemeanour had sprung the Rugby game. We never investigated him, being ashamed of even this peripheral connection with a game where they cheered like mad every time you kicked the ball OFF the field, but we did know about him, and we did know that there were versions of football other than our own.

In 1944 a catastrophe occurred. SMGS, having disrupted Cornish life to its own satisfaction, returned home to claim its sons, including me, which meant that I, a dedicated centre half, was now expected to play with an egg-shaped ball, wear boots with bars instead of studs, and persistently handle the ball. In the end, being large for my age, I was shoved at the back of the First XV scrum, from which vantage point I soon acquired a worm's-eye view of the world which was not congenial to me. I was then moved out to the wing and my soccer skills utilised in the matter of place kicks, in which I became something of a specialist and only ever trod on my scrum half once. (In those days conversion kicks had to be taken with your scrum half in a recumbent posture, holding the ball off the ground and quaking.)

Our fifteen was representative of the school generally. That is to say, we went through the 1945-46 season with a hundred per cent record, losing every game. There was a close call one afternoon at Raynes Park, who beat us by a try to nil, and I recall one Saturday when we actually avoided defeat. We were without a fixture owing to the mental instability of the Games Master, so we all went off to see the Wasps play a Welsh side which included a man called Bleddyn Williams. I think it was that same season that a few of us went to watch a pickup side called London Counties get hammered by the New Zealand tourists, one of whose players, a full back called Scott, dropped a goal from just inside his own half. This made me a bit thoughtful, and the following Wednesday I dropped one against Kilburn Grammar from well inside theirs. Again, this was the season when I first realised that there is such a thing as a scrum half's physique, short bandy legs, dropped hips, broad shoulders and that low centre of gravity which enables a man to keep running even though someone twice his weight is sitting on his head.

As this essay is sure to be scrutinised by Rugby's most powerful intellects, this is probably the moment for me to disclose for the very first time the fact that in that 1945-46 season I made a brilliantly original contribution to the tactics of the game, a contribution which was unjustly spurned at the time and labelled as Ungentlemanly Conduct by our Games Master, who incidentally wouldn't have recognised Gentlemanly Conduct if a lorryload of it had been tipped over him. One midweek

afternoon we went over to south London to play a rival school, and found ourselves turned inside out by their right wing threequarter, whose mother had clearly been having an affair with a stag. He was such a flier that he had only to gain possession to streak over our line. After forty minutes we were losing 21-0. Clearly the only way to avoid a rout was to nobble the flier. The problem was that he was so fast that you couldn't get close enough to tackle him. It was then I came up with my idea.

Bringing all my Holmesian powers to bear on the problem, I formulated the following conclusions: that he could only be handled if slowed down, that he could only be slowed down if winded, that he could only be winded if tackled, that he could only be tackled if you happened to be standing next to him at the exact moment when he started to run. But if you simply followed him about, the referee would be sure to blow up for offside or some such technicality. There was only one thing for it, and it surprised me, decades later, when the All Blacks so feebly failed to think of it when confronted by Barry John. When the second half started, I received the ball, ran across the field, straight to the enemy gazelle, and tossed the ball to him. No sooner had it landed in his stupefied arms than I jumped on him, for was he not a legitimate target? Was he not in possession? Was I not onside? Anyway, there was a big argument after that, and the referee

warned me not to break the rules. I asked him which rule I was breaking, and he, giving a typical schoolmaster's reply, told me not to be insolent. We lost 48-0 that afternoon and honour was satisfied, even at the cost of one of the most imaginative ploys ever conceived.

Since those days my attitude has mellowed somewhat. I think Cliff Morgan had something to do with it, because there was no denying the wonderful grace of his touch-kicking when running towards his own goal, the half-turn and the ball flung down on to his own boot. Then there was the genius of John, a genius so blatant that even I could see it. And then the transmission of internationals on BBC television. And then watching my own sons play the game. And the day they dragged me to Twickenham. And the day it dawned on me that as my mother's family comes from Yorkshire, and as all the members of that family took Rugby League seriously, then my allegiance to the Union game could be my revenge. One last point. I recall that just after the invention of the tactical departure described above, I was writing a history essay. Curious to plumb the precise depths of ignorance of our teachers, I wrote that Prince Obolensky was generally believed to have been deeply implicated in the assassination of Rasputin. They marked me up at 68 out of a hundred.

And that, I believe, was how I came to be an expert on the subject of Rugby Union.

Rugby at grass roots. The shorts have got shorter since this match between Harrow and the Merchant Taylors, but the adjoining pitches, the winter trees, the clumpy grass and the small knots of spectators are all still familiar to modern players.

The Evolution of Rugby

Stephen Jones

The legend has it that rugby was 'invented' by a pupil at Rugby School called William Webb Ellis. During a game of football in 1823 on Big Side, the school's playing field, he picked up the ball and ran towards the opposition goal line with it. Hence, in an instant, a revolutionary new game appeared. Of course, history rarely lends itself to such cut and dried presentation. Rugby evolved, it was not invented. Ellis infringed the rules of a sport and perhaps hastened the development of another but rugby sprang from several sorts of game, took in over a long period several differing influences and eventually emerged as a pastime bearing a resemblance to the game of today.

One of the earliest ancestors of rugby was harpastum, a game played by the Romans, and there are also parallels between the sport and the 'town games', in which an inflated pig's bladder was borne through the town by two teams, the object being to take it to a given point in the town and also prevent the opposition taking it to another given point. These points were the forerunners of goal lines.

Even though cold water must be poured on the notion that Webb Ellis was the inventor of rugby, there is no doubt whatever that Rugby School, and the other major public schools like Charterhouse and Winchester, played a vital role in developing the sport. In the early 19th century there were still several variations of the football game. The type of game which each school played often depended on what ground facilities were available. Those establishments with paved areas favoured a dribbling game, those with large grassy areas preferred the scrummage of the handling game – in fact, this is a most important distinction. The dribbling game evolved into soccer and the handling game into rugby.

Some of the games were peculiar to one school only – the Eton wall game is one of the few which survives, one of the few which refused to be unified into a single game, a single set of rules. In the mid-19th

Above *The man who allegedly started the rugby code of football in later life became the Rev. W. W. Ellis, M.A.*

Right *The school after which rugby was named. The master, ladies and child strolling across the playing fields of Rugby seem to be taking it all rather lightly.*

century, the most important aspect of the largest of the 'rugby-like' games was the maul, in which almost any number from each side would push and strain in a large, crabbing mass in an endeavour to make ground towards the opposition goal line. Once a touchdown had been made, a try for goal, or conversion was allowed, and if the goal went over, the scorer would be in the lead by one goal to nil. That try for goal which a touchdown allowed has now come to have value in itself. Touchdowns are now called tries! Eventually, running with the ball in the manner of Ellis was allowed, since it was a more attractive and effective means of scoring than the protracted maul.

Nothing was more certain than that the game would spread to the universities at Cambridge and Oxford. The old pupils of the major schools soon caused the spread of the game to Oxbridge, and gradually sets of rules which unified the different codes were produced. In the second half of the 19th century, University clubs sprang up, followed by clubs at the teaching hospitals and, eventually, town clubs like Blackheath and Bradford, Liverpool and Harlequins. In 1863, those proponents of the dribbling game formed the Football Association and eight years later, in 1871, the handling code set up its own governing body, the Rugby Football Union, with 21 clubs represented on the original body.

The Rugby Union was now able to end the confusion of differing laws and practices and provide a focal point for the game in England. But the formation of the new body did even more than that – within two months of its formation, the Rugby Union put out an England team to do battle with a Scottish team in the first-ever rugby international. On 7 March 1871, at Raeburn Place in Edinburgh, Scotland defeated England and nothing was more natural than a return match. England duly exacted revenge a year later by beating Scotland at Kennington Oval in London, and the series of matches which is now known as the International Championship was inaugurated. Ireland, Wales and, later, France joined in and rugby union's most prestigious competition began a steady growth in stature.

Although Scotland was already playing international matches its own governing body was not established until 1893. Six clubs, namely Glasgow Academicals, Royal High School Former Pupils, Merchistonians, West of Scotland, Edinburgh University and Edinburgh Academicals, sat down and formed the union and the game quickly spread in the country with the border clubs becoming particularly strong. A feature of the early years of Scottish rugby which, generally speaking, is still applicable is that their clubs tended to be old boys' teams. Many people believe that this system had held back the development of a successful Scottish national side. Nevertheless, since Scotland challenged England to that first international match in 1871, the Scots can justly claim to be the originators of the rugby international.

A match from 1871, the year the Rugby Football Union was formed. This picture by E. Buckman was called 'The Last Scrummage' – perhaps the match was about to disintegrate into violence, as one or two fists appear clenched.

'A good run, but collared' was the caption on this 1877 rugby illustration. The teams could still play each other today, for the match was the Hospital Challenge Cup Final, with Guy's playing St. Thomas's.

The next of the four home countries to form a coherent governing body was Ireland and, once again, student teams played an enormous part in the formation of the Irish Rugby Union and in the development of the game generally. There is conclusive evidence that Dublin University had a rugby side in the 1850s and the large schools and universities followed by forming their own teams shortly afterwards. Although the Union was not formed until 1879, Ireland began playing England in international games as early as 1875 and since then, although Ireland has rarely proved invincible opposition, the contribution which the country has made to the game on and off the field is remarkable. Many of rugby's 'characters' are Irish.

Wales has been such a leader in the game, such a success playing-wise and such an innovator, that it comes as a surprise to learn that the Welsh Rugby Union was not

One of the greatest three-quarters of the 1890s was a man who also captained England at cricket. Blackheath's A. E. Stoddart was known for his method of leaping into the air to avoid tackles.

'The last pass' – a painting by Ernest Prater. Disaster is about to overcome the Reds, as the ball should go out to the wing three-quarter, who can hardly fail to score.

International rugby in 1893. Oxford University played the Racing Club of France, at Becon-les-Bruyères, in Paris and according to the report 'impressed the spectators . . . by their fine physique and vigorous appearance, no member of the team being less than six feet in height.' Oxford won by two goals and a try to nil.

formed until 1881. The reasons for this become clear if one returns to the origins of the game. Wales had fewer public schools than England, fewer contacts with the developing areas of the game. Rugby in Wales was not based on old boys' teams or universities, but on town clubs like Cardiff and Swansea, Newport and Neath. Although this saw Wales slightly slower off the mark in rugby development, it eventually became a great strength of the game. Today, the great town clubs are the basis of the success of the game in Wales.

At the start of the 20th century, the series of matches between the big clubs and the major touring sides began, and once again, this series still continues today with Newport, Llanelli, Cardiff and Swansea proud

A drawing by S. T. Dadd of a match at Blackheath in 1897. It is difficult to believe there was ever a more convincing hand-off since.

holders of several illustrious scalps.

The basis of early Welsh rugby was its classlessness. Whereas in England and Scotland the public schoolboys and past pupils played the game, in Wales one did not have to be a member of the social elite to play. Once again, this fact may have hindered the early development of the game in Wales but it did the on-field success of Welsh teams no harm at all.

With rugby thriving in Britain, with the new clubs and the codified rules, the next step was the spread of the game overseas, but before the end of the 19th century there was an upheaval in the domestic scene, a sign that rugby was experiencing severe growing pains. The pains were particularly in the North of England, where the game tended to be played by the working classes, as in Wales.

Some of the Northern clubs found that rugby was taking up an increasing amount of their players' time and often causing them to miss work. Their demands to the Rugby Union that broken time payments should be made to compensate those who lost money to play rugby fell on stony ground and, as is explained more fully later, the Northern Union, later the Rugby League, came into being and broke completely, not only with the Rugby Union in London, but with the game of rugby union itself.

Returning to the spread of the game around the world it is once again fair to give a lot of the credit to public schoolboys. With their education over, many left for foreign lands, either on business or in the armed forces, and nothing was more certain that they would carry on their rugby traditions overseas. The rise of rugby union in those scores of countries who play the game can usually be traced directly to British men of commerce or of the forces introducing disbelieving natives to the wonders of the oval ball. In South Africa, rugby clubs were formed as early as the 1880s. A British exile, C. J. Monro, cultivated the germ of rugby in New Zealand and started the process by which it became the national sport. Wine merchants from Britain introduced the French to the game and colonists from Britain took rugby as far afield as Australia. Even today, with rugby union booming and being played in more than 100 countries, a visiting British ship, or even an individual, can provide a spark to enrapture a nation.

Famous Rugby Union Clubs

Stephen Jones

In this chapter on famous clubs, 16 from around 200 first-class British clubs are dealt with, chosen not just on the basis of historical excellence, but also with an eye to recent successes.

BRISTOL

Year of foundation: 1888
Ground: Memorial Ground, Filton Avenue, Horfield, Bristol
Colours: Blue and white hoops
It is too much of a generalisation to say that, of the two great West Country rivals, Bristol have traditionally provided attractive rugby whereas Gloucester, their near neighbours, have produced forward power play, but, as a rule, the brand of rugby served up by Bristol has been based largely on skill behind the scrum and on the efforts of some of the great forwards of England rugby.

The club was formed by the amalgamation of Carlton and Redland and the ground, though on the site of their present home, the Memorial Ground, was known as Buffalo Bill's Field. At a match to open the new Memorial Ground in 1921, a vast crowd gathered to watch Bristol defeat Cardiff. The late 1920s and late 1960s were among the most successful eras in the club's history.

In the 1980s the club is not quite achieving the results which the talent of the players at its disposal might suggest, although, at home especially, they never provide anything less than formidable opposition. Probably their most famous player of the modern era has been Dave Rollitt, the 'Grey Fox' of the back row, who caused problems for the opposition in two decades.

BRIDGEND

Year of formation: 1878
Ground: Brewery Field, Tondu Road, Bridgend
Colours: Blue and white stripes
Although the club was officially formed in 1878 there are conclusive records that many matches were played in the town before this date. The main problem which the club has encountered is the continual changing of headquarters. It actually moved to the Brewery Field after the First World War but then the Field was purchased by a greyhound racing operation and later, after dog racing had ceased and Bridgend returned, by a rugby league syndicate making a last and eventually, ill-fated attempt to establish the game in South Wales. The club had a nomadic existence until 1958, when the Brewery Field was once again leased to them, this time a long lease!

Billy Delahay and Vivian Jenkins have been two of the club's most famous players and they set a tradition which the club of today has faithfully followed. They were Welsh cup winners in 1979 and 1980 and losing finalists a year later.

BALLYMENA

Year of formation: 1922
Ground: Eaton Park, Ballymena
Colours: Black
Ballymena can claim as a true son of the club one of the greatest men in rugby in Willie-John McBride, who won 63 Irish caps, led the most successful Lions party in history (to South Africa in 1974) and whose fierce character on the field, and appealing modesty off it, has made him a much-loved figure.

Ballymena is traditionally the strongest side in the Ulster Senior League with some of its best seasons coming in the mid-1970s, with McBride's influence being important even though, due to his pressing representative commitments, he was unable to play in many games. Yet as the 1980s wore on the club was having difficulty maintaining its proud record, no doubt a trough before the next run of success.

CARDIFF

Year of formation: 1876
Ground: Cardiff Arms Park, Westgate Street, Cardiff
Colours: Blue and black hoops
The achievements of the Cardiff club could fill several books, with their formidable line of Welsh caps and outstanding contribution to all aspects of the game in Wales. Players like Gwyn Nicholls, Percy Bush, Wilfred Wooller, Haydn Tanner, Jack Matthews, Bleddyn Williams, Gareth Edwards, Barry John, and now Terry Holmes and Gareth Davies have a place in any hall of rugby fame. Best of all, most of Cardiff's

achievements on the field have come about due to a brand of open, attacking football with the emphasis on the backs and rarely has a Cardiff team taken the field in its history without at least one world-class performer behind the scrum.

Cardiff's record against the major touring sides is spectacular. They have beaten the Maoris, South Africa (twice), New Zealand, and Australia (four times). For a club to have caused the world's great teams such problems is an indication of its stature.

CORK CONSTITUTION

Year of foundation: 1894
Ground: Temple Hill, Cork
Colours: Blue, black and white hoops

There can be very few clubs which were founded by members of the media, but Cork Constitution was the name of a newspaper whose staff helped found the club. The famous rugby family Murphy, which includes Lions coach Noel, has usually been represented in the club by the holding of one office or another and Cork Constitution has been traditionally one of Ireland's strongest clubs.

Tom Kiernan, coach to the Irish national squad which won the 1982 International

Championship, is the club's most capped player and was a magnificent full-back who also led the 1968 British Lions party which toured South Africa. In fact, with commendable continuity, Kiernan took over as Irish coach from Noel Murphy and guided the side to the 1982 Triple Crown.

COVENTRY

Year of formation: 1874
Ground: Coundon Road, Coventry
Colours: Navy blue and white hoops
There are signs that, in the 1980s, Coventry, one of England's greatest clubs, are re-awakening and returning to their former eminence after a long period in which their results bore little relation to the standing of the club. Their achievement in reaching a John Player Cup semi-final in 1982 provides evidence that players like Huw Davies, Tim Buttimore and Graham Robbins can restore former glories.

For many years the club has been a real power base of English rugby and there was a local axiom that when Coventry were good, England were good. From Coventry, players like Alan Rotherham, Ivor Preece, and Peter Jackson have been launched on international

careers, and in Jackson and David Duckham, the idol of Coventry in the 1970s, the club has provided arguably the outstanding post-war wings in the country.

Since they won two John Player Cup finals in succession in 1973 and 1974, Coventry have found the going tough and taken a back seat to the success of their great Midland rivals, Leicester. The happy event of their renaissance was only marred by the passing in 1982 of Alf Wyman, their former secretary and one of rugby's greatest administrators.

GALA

Year of formation: 1876
Ground: Netherdale, Galashiels
Colours: Maroon
Fittingly, the first ever match undertaken by Gala was against Hawick, in 1876 and 'start as you mean to go on' was undoubtedly the motto of the day because the pair have been close rivals ever since. After an unmemorable first season, Gala had a further setback when a section of the membership broke away to form another club, taking away Gala's precious goalposts!

Jock Wemyss, J. H. Ferguson, George Bur-

Opposite top Steve Fenwick and J. P. R. Williams (with ball) playing for Bridgend when they won the Welsh Cup Final in 1979.

Opposite below Colin Murphy gets a pass away for a Cork Constitution side playing against Bill Beaumont's XV, for whom Colin Tucker is doing the chasing.

Below Coventry playing Gloucester in the John Player Cup semi-final of 1982. Phil Blakeway, Gloucester's England forward, is leading the charge.

rell, Norman Bruce, Jim Aitken and David Leslie are among the many internationals produced by the club with Aitken's finest hour coming when he led his side to the Scottish league titles in 1980 and 1981, thereby breaking the domination of Hawick in that competition.

GLOUCESTER

Year of formation: 1873
Ground: Kingsholm, Kingsholm Road, Gloucester
Colours: Cherry and white hoops

No club inspires more devotion from its supporters or more passion and loyalty from its players than Gloucester. The city and its surrounds is rugby country – in fact, Gloucester is one of the largest cities in England without a soccer club in the Football League. The result is that the rugby team is part of a real town club with which people in the locality can readily identify.

From the club's formation it provided harsh opposition and indeed, very few teams in history have arrived at Kingsholm relishing the old-fashioned Gloucester welcome!

The late Tom Voyce, a successful RFU president in 1960, is one of the club's most famous figures as player and administrator while the forward power at the club has since been assisted by the likes of Peter Ford, Mike Nicholls, Mike Burton and Phil Blakeway. Yet at present, with the club probably the strongest overall in England, there is a move afoot in the team to bring the backs more into the game, which can only improve the image and success of a great club.

GOSFORTH

Year of formation: 1877
Ground: New Ground, Great North Road, Gosforth, Newcastle
Colours: Green and white hoops

Gosforth are not one of the great clubs of English rugby history. They have no long record of providing players or administrators for England, no protracted success down through the decades such as that which Coventry or Gloucester can boast. Yet any discussion of the leading clubs nowadays must include the Geordie club. In the 1970s they built a superb team around some of the outstanding forwards of the era, especially British Lions Peter Dixon and Roger Uttley, and around their efficient scrum-half, Malcolm Young.

For once, the soccer city of Newcastle had its attention drawn from St James Park as Gosforth won the John Player Cup finals of 1975 and 1976. They beat Waterloo 23-14 in the former and Rosslyn Park 27-11 in the latter.

The success of Gosforth, maintained in the 1980s though in a lesser key, has broadened the power base of English rugby to the extent that the Northumberland county team, based on the club, is now one of the strongest county sides.

HAWICK

Year of formation: 1873
Ground: Mansfield Park, Hawick
Colours: Green

Hawick was one of the earliest clubs formed in Scotland which was not a former pupils' institution. It was formed as a branch of a cricket club, and in his book 'Great Rugger Clubs', J. B. G. (Bryn) Thomas, doyen of rugby writers, records that early Hawick rugby matches took place without touch lines and goalposts!

Things have changed, because nowadays few people could dispute that Hawick is the leading club in Scotland, providing internationals like Jim Renwick, Colin Deans and Alan Tomes and dominating the Scottish League Division One. Since the leagues started in 1973, Hawick has been dominant. The club won six titles out of nine, with only its great rivals in the Scottish Borders, Gala, winning the title more than once apart from them.

LEICESTER

Year of formation: 1880
Ground: Welford Road, Leicester
Colours: Scarlet, green and white hoops

The grip which Leicester, the famous Tigers, held on English club rugby has only recently been loosened. They reached every John Player Cup final between 1978 and 1981 inclusive, played some sparkling, quality rugby during that time and provided full-back Dusty Hare, centres Paul Dodge and Clive Woodward, fly-half Les Cusworth and hooker Peter Wheeler for the England side. In fact, all five played for England in the same match twice in the 1982 international season and nowhere is Leicester's contribution to the modern game better emphasised than in the fact that they provided a third of the England side. History will judge Dodge, Wheeler and club coach Chalky White as

It's a long way from Pontypool to the Bay of Plenty, New Zealand, but the famous Pontypool front row of Price, Windsor and Faulkner went on to play together for the Lions there.

among the most influential rugby men of the era.

The original Leicester side was a representative team of local clubs. Compare the club's first annual income of less than two pounds with the gate receipts which their thousands of loyal fans generate at every home match at Welford Road.

Leicester have enjoyed several successful eras, though none approaches the success of recent years. They are one of very few clubs to be granted an annual fixture with the famous Barbarians.

LLANELLI

Year of formation: 1872
Ground: Stradey Park, Llanelli
Colours: Scarlet

There is little doubt that the greatest day in the proud history of Llanelli, the famous West Wales 'Scarlets', came in 1972 when thousands of people crammed into Stradey Park and watched their heroes beat Ian Kirkpatrick's All Blacks. It was a typical Llanelli victory, based on sheer passion from the forwards and the traditional skill behind the scrum. Captain Delme Thomas, it was said, gave such an emotional team talk to his men before the game, that many of the Llanelli players were in tears.

Llanelli first announced their growing strength in 1882 when they won the South Wales Challenge Cup and six years later they beat the Maoris. The club soon produced one of the greatest centres in history in Rhys Gabe, who struck up a memorable partnership at international level with Gwyn Nicholls. Albert Jenkins, Ivor Jones, Bill Clement, Rhys Williams and later, Delme Thomas, Phil Bennett, Derek Quinnell and Ray Gravell have all served Wales well after learning their trade at one of the world's most fervent clubs.

MOSELEY

Year of foundation: 1873
Ground: The Reddings, Reddings Road, Moseley, Birmingham 13
Colours: Black and red hoops

Moseley was formed as a branch of the Havelock cricket club, whose members wished for a diversion to pass the long winter months until wickets could be pitched again. With a membership of 20, the rugby club struggled in its first season but eventually developed into a giant of Midland rugby with a golden era in the 1920s and the 1970s. Earlier, the club were invincible for three seasons between 1879 and 1882.

J. F. Byrne was an early Moseley hero, playing at full-back for the club for many seasons, for England 13 times and for the British Lions in South Africa in 1896, and among the more modern Moseley stars have been Peter Cranmer and Peter Robbins. The outstanding figures in Moseley's memorable form of the

1970s were Martin Cooper, a fly-half who converted to full-back, Jan Webster, the tough scrum-half, and locks Nigel Horton and Barry Ayre.

Moseley never captured public affection as Leicester have done, not surprisingly, given the huge competition of soccer in the Birmingham area, but an appearance in the 1982 John Player Cup final proved that playing-wise, the club is as strong as ever.

NEWPORT

Year of formation: 1875
Ground: Rodney Parade, Rodney Road, Newport
Colours: Black and amber hoops

The fact that Newport are hardly setting the rugby world alight at the moment should not obscure the fact that this is one of the greatest of all rugby clubs and that the lead Newport has given to the playing and administrative sides of the game may well be unequalled. The club has enjoyed six invincible seasons while no other Welsh club has achieved more than one. It has provided internationals for all four home countries and for South Africa and once fielded a team, for a match against Bristol, which was all international, and there were three other caps in reserve. Furthermore, Newport has beaten New Zealand, Australia, and South Africa and was the only side to defeat the formidable Fifth All Blacks in 1963. Even the invincible All Blacks of 1924 reckoned that they were lucky to escape defeat at Rodney Parade.

Arthur Gould, the prince of three-quarters, was the game's first true 'superstar'. Jerry Shea, Jack Wetter, Bunner Travers, Jack Morley, Alf Panting, Bryn Meredith, David Watkins, Brian Price, Alan Dobbins, Keith Jarrett – all these great players are Newport men and part of the rugby hall of fame.

A famous Rosslyn Park player from the past, Prince Obolensky, tackles an Old Blues player in a 1936 encounter.

The green and white hoops of Gosforth on the back of their British Lion Roger Uttley.

Andy Ripley, Rosslyn Park's best-known player of recent years, being checked by a London Welsh tackle in the middle of one of his long-striding runs.

PONTYPOOL

Year of formation: 1901
Ground: Pontypool Park, Pontypool
Colours: Red, white and black hoops

The Eastern Valley club is not among the traditional Welsh 'big four' of Cardiff, Llanelli, Swansea and Newport, but that has not deterred it from upsetting the traditional powers frequently. From the early 1970s, Pontypool has developed forward power that any other club in the world can only envy. Schooled by Ray Prosser, the former British Lions prop, forwards like Bobby Windsor, Tony Faulkner, Graham Price, Terry Cobner and, on joining from Newport, Jeff Squire, have combined in fearsome fashion.

The Pontypool front row of Windsor, Faulkner and Price played as a unit for Wales and the Lions and have become almost legendary. Price has proved probably Wales' greatest prop forward in history.

The forerunner of the Pontypool club was Pontymoel, but once the town team of Pontypool had been established, progress was swift. By 1913, Pontypool had become Welsh champions and from then until the present, a succession of formidable packs have kept 'Ponty' on top.

ROSSLYN PARK

Year of formation: 1879
Ground: Roehampton, Upper Richmond Road, London SW 15
Colours: Red and white hoops

The Park have always managed to keep a praiseworthy perspective on rugby and on the follies of playing to win at all costs. With close ties with Oxbridge and the Services their traditional strength was assured, even if the development of a really formidable team is a rare feat for them. Once again, the rugby club sprang from the desire of cricketers to while away the cold winter months, but Rosslyn Park rugby club quickly overhauled the Rosslyn Park cricket club in stature and membership.

Like all London clubs, the Park has suffered from a certain lack of identity – the lot of all clubs in the large cities which have their resources diluted by the demands of competing clubs, but very few English clubs in history have consistently got the better of Park.

No-one epitomises the effective but ultimately sporting and chivalrous approach of the club better than Andy Ripley, their former England and British Lion No 8 and one of the most popular figures amongst team and supporters that rugby union has ever thrown up.

Great Union Players

David Norrie

Bill Beaumont

The revival of English rugby in the late 1970s had popular lock and leader Bill Beaumont at its head. He looked a certainty to become the first man ever to lead two British Lions' tour, but his career was cut short by injury during the 1982 Championship. Beaumont received a bang on the head during the county championship final and was advised that any further knocks might have serious consequences; so, regrettably, he called it a day. It was a sad end to a fine career which had blossomed on the Lions' trip of 1977 when he was flown out as a replacement, yet fought his way into the Test team. He'd captained England in 1978, and after Roger Uttley's

Bill Beaumont, with headband, in a line-out for England against Wales in 1978, the year in which he took over the England captaincy.

Above *Ken Catchpole of Australia, in no danger from a despairing tackle from a rival scrum-half, gets his pass away during the 1966 Australian tour of Britain.*

Opposite top *One of the most successful kickers in the history of rugby, All Black Don Clarke puts over another conversion.*

Opposite below *Typical Gerald Davies action – the fast run, the hand-off, perhaps another Welsh try on the way.*

regret about his career was that it was ended abruptly and prematurely.

Ken Catchpole skippered Australia on his début, at the age of 21, against the South Africans in 1961, but it was when he teamed up with fly-half Phil Hawthorne in 1963 that his reputation became worldwide. The pair made a tremendous impact during the Wallabies' tour of Britain in 1966; the highlights being victories over Wales and England, with Hawthorne dropping a hat-trick of goals in the latter match.

That partnership was split up when Hawthorne went to play league rugby the following year and, sadly, Catchpole's career was also nearing its end. In his 24th match for Australia, he found himself trapped in a ruck. All Black Colin Meads, in his efforts to get to the ball, grabbed Catchpole's free leg and pulled. Like a chicken wishbone, the muscles tore and the crack could be heard all over the ground. It was a tragic ending to a rare footballing talent.

Don Clarke

New Zealand's full-back Don Clarke used his feared right boot to become the greatest match-winner in rugby history. By the time that boot was finally hung up, it had claimed 201 points for the All Blacks in 34 Tests, then a world record.

Clarke burst upon the international scene in 1956 when his kicking clinched New Zealand's first series win over South Africa for 19 years. For the next eight years Clarke was a feared and respected All Black, establishing himself as much a villain to some as he was a hero to others. His most notorious afternoon came on 18 July 1959 when his six penalty goals left the Lions 18-17 losers, despite four fine British tries. There was even talk of lowering the value of the penalty goal to counter his immense threat.

In the ensuing years, Clarke's gift was to be seen on the rugby fields of South Africa, Australia, Britain and France – and everywhere he went, his impact was amazing. Only during the tour of Britain did his kicking touch desert him for the first time in his long international career; but while off kicking form he demonstrated that his boot had overshadowed some of the other footballing talents of this solidly-built Kiwi.

second, brief spell as skipper, Beaumont returned to lead England until his retirement. That was a total of 21 games in charge, easily an English record and he was to skipper sides to victories against all the other major countries. His most memorable season was 1979-80. After leading the North to a conclusive 21-9 success over the All Blacks, he was at the head of England's first Grand Slam for 23 years before taking the Lions to South Africa. He proved a most popular leader and his side should have won the series, given their undoubted forward superiority. In his 33rd and penultimate appearance for England, Australia were the victims to complete his set of scalps. His departure cast a shadow over the 1982 Championship, but rugby people everywhere were glad that Bill Beaumont was still around to enjoy his memories.

Ken Catchpole

The 1960s produced a glut of world-class scrum-halves – Gareth Edwards, Chris Laidlow and Sid Going among others. Yet the player rated by many experts to be the best was an Australian, Ken Catchpole. He had a lightning quick pass, but it was his shrewd rugby brain and tactical awareness that helped make him an exceptional player. Catchpole was able to take control, even amongst the finest company; the only

Danie Craven

Despite the fact that he is past 70, Danie Craven is still the most influential man in South African rugby. To many he is 'Mr Rugby'. His early fame was based on his dive pass from scrum-half, which was new to the game, and he came over, uncapped, on Benny Osler's tour of Britain. He quickly made his name as a wet-weather scrum-half and rather unfairly this tag remained with him. Craven had the perfect build for the number nine jersey, short and stocky, rather reminiscent of Gareth Edwards. He remained in the Springbok team until the outbreak of war, helping the South Africans to that historic triumph in New Zealand in 1937 and, the following year, captained his country to victory over the Lions. Though only 27, he retired after 16 caps, with three of those games being out of position at fly-half, centre and No. 8.

Craven later coached before becoming South Africa's leading administrator. He is also an influential figure on the Inter-

Mervyn Davies, one of the best British forwards of recent times, leading out the Barbarians, whom he captained in their match against Australia in 1976.

mare. He enhanced all the teams he played for – Cardiff, London Welsh, Loughborough Colleges, Wales, the Barbarians, Cambridge University and the British Lions; he especially became a favourite of the crowd at the Middlesex Sevens.

He made his début in the centre for Wales, aged 21, in the 1966 defeat by Australia, but it wasn't until he moved to the wing during Wales' tour of New Zealand and Australia that he found his true niche. Davies ran in five tries during Wales' 1971 Grand Slam season, including the score that allowed John Taylor to hit that left-footed conversion which defeated the Scots 19-18. His influence on the 1971 Lions was just as great and his try in the opening minutes of the third Test was the crucial score in clinching that series.

Davies was unavailable for the Lions' tour of 1974 and 1977, but he returned home to Wales to captain Cardiff. His final year was another Grand Slam one for Wales and, at the beginning of the 1978-79 season, despite being elected to lead Cardiff for a third term, he decided to call it a day after 45 caps and 20 tries for Wales. Immediately, he was missed and, as yet, British rugby awaits a replacement to take his place.

national Board where he has tried to retain South Africa's position, despite the fact that the country has been isolated on many sporting fronts because of its apartheid policies. As yet there's no end to that situation in sight, but Doctor Craven is willing to carry on the battles as long as is necessary.

Gerald Davies

Gerald Davies belongs to that rare breed of players whose talents transcend time and place – he would have been a great player in any era. Davies formed the main attraction of Wales and Britain in the late 1960s and 1970s – crowds would buzz with excitement whenever he got the ball and he seldom disappointed them. Davies could jink and side-step at speed and his deadly acceleration made him a defender's night-

Mervyn Davies

Mervyn Davies was the outstanding post-war British forward, but may have missed his finest hour through no fault of his own. He was struck down by a brain haemorrhage in a cup semi-final just after he had led Wales to the 1976 Grand Slam; thankfully, he survived, but he never took the field again and was thus denied his right – the captaincy of the 1977 British Lions to New Zealand. They never recovered from his absence and Wales, especially, took a lot of time to re-style their game without him. 'Merv the Swerve' had been an ever-present in the Welsh side since his début, along with J. P. R. Williams, in the 1969 game against Scotland. His 38 caps were all consecutive and he played in all the Tests on the British Lions tours of 1971 and 1974, only losing once in these eight matches. He skippered Wales in his last nine internationals and again was on the losing side on only one occasion. While Davies's talents were manifold, it was his ability as a ball-winner, both at set pieces and set phase, which was

his outstanding feature. He formed a telepathic understanding with scrum-half Gareth Edwards – the pair were together in all Davies's games for Wales and the Lions – and their finest hour came with Mc-Bride's Lions in South Africa in 1974 when they toyed with the Springbok loose forwards. Half his caps were won with London Welsh – he was one of seven representatives with that club who were 1971 Lions – and the other half with Swansea, where he ended his career.

David Duckham

It was a pity to England's rugby supporters that their most exciting back of recent years, David Duckham, always seemed to be given the opportunities to show off his immense skills in sides other than the national team. Perhaps his most memor-

able performance was given in a Barbarians' jersey in their 1973 classic encounter against Ian Kirkpatrick's All Blacks. Now he had the multi-talented players around him and he responded to the challenge with some of the most devastating and unpredictable running ever seen on a rugby field.

His days with England were not so happy; fourteen of his 36 caps were won in the centre, the rest on the wing. His early days were spent as one half of a midfield combination with John Spencer, but when the latter lost favour, Duckham moved to the wing. England were going through a torrid time and it was rare for him to find the same players inside him for more than a couple of games at a time. All of this was not conducive to giving him the chances his talent deserved and so many of his international afternoons were wasted.

A determined Van Wyk of North Transvaal attempts to lay hands on Gareth Edwards, playing for the Lions in South Africa in 1974. Mervyn Davies has his eye on the situation.

One of the best and most versatile of rugby players, Mike Gibson, coming away with the ball and plenty of Irish support in a match against England.

Slams. He captained Wales at the tender age of 20 – a figure he matched in the number of tries he scored for Wales. Edwards was strong, a brilliant tactical kicker and a scrum-half who overcame a weak service to develop one of the finest and longest spin passes ever seen in the game. He formed two legendary half-back partnerships – the first with Barry John, a pairing which also starred for the 1971 Lions – the second with Phil Bennett, the benefit of which was also shared by the 1974 Lions.

Edwards was devastating near the line, but the two tries for which he is best remembered were rather different. Against Scotland he raced nearly the length of the field, chipped ahead and just won the race to the ball before it slithered over the deadball line. The following winter, it was Edwards who put the finishing touches on the Barbarians' opening try against the All Blacks which Phil Bennett had started with those audacious side-steps near his own line.

He did enjoy, though, being part of the Lions' success in New Zealand in 1971 and he was to enjoy further success against the All Blacks other than the Barbarians' victory. He had earlier led Midland Counties West to an historic win on that tour and in 1973 was in the England team that surprised and defeated New Zealand in Auckland. Towards the end of his career, he was plagued by injury and his condition could not have been helped by the fact that he was on the winning side in only six of his last 25 games for England.

Gareth Edwards

Gareth Edwards was the dominant rugby personality of the 1970s and even after he retired in 1978 he carried on breaking records, with his autobiography becoming one of the biggest-selling sporting books of all time. From his début against France in 1967 until Wales' Grand Slam victory over the same opponents in 1978, Edwards played 53 consecutive games for his country, an amazing feat for somebody playing scrum-half, where the physical rigours are intense.

His records did not end there – Wales lost only once at Cardiff during his 12-year tenancy and claimed many championships and Triple Crowns as well as three Grand

Mike Gibson

Mike Gibson is probably the most complete footballer seen since the Second World War – he could play equally well at fly-half or centre and, in fact, towards the end of his career played a few matches on the wing for Ireland. Gibson went on five British Lions tours – a record he holds along with Willie John McBride – and made his final appearances for Ireland when he came out of retirement in 1979 to help them to their famous 2-0 victory in Australia.

Mike Gibson had first given warning of his immense capabilities with Cambridge University in the early 1960s and he was soon in the Irish side. He was to remain there from 1964 until 1979, winning 69 caps in the process – a world record – and that doesn't include his twelve appearances in Tests for the British Lions. Those early days were spent at fly-half, where he showed a shrewd tactical awareness. When he was injured in 1969, a newcomer, Barry McGann, was introduced and he played so well he could not realistically be dropped. So Gibson moved to the centre and the second phase of his career began. The 1971 British Lions' tour of New Zealand saw Gibson play his finest rugby; he was selected as one of the two fly-halves, but everybody knew that Barry John would play there and Gibson would be in the centre. It is interesting to note that Colin Meads rated Gibson the reason, along with Mervyn Davies, for the Lions' success in that Test series.

Andy Irvine

From the moment he made his début against the All Blacks in 1972, it was obvious to everyone that Scotland had found in Andy Irvine a full-back in keeping with their fine traditions. He was to remain on the international scene for a decade, breaking goal-scoring, try-scoring and appearances records as he went along. In later years, he skippered Scotland, who in the early 1980s were becoming a major force in the championship. Although sometimes casual and absent-minded in defence, he could turn disaster into triumph with one of his brilliant breaks. Irvine toured with the British Lions in 1974, 1977 and 1980, often overcoming a shaky start to find his best form. On that first tour, particularly, he emerged to force his way in the Test side and ended up with 156 points, a record. By the end of the 1982 championship, Irvine had played 49 times for his country, only one behind the Scottish record held by Sandy Carmichael, and his points tally was well on its way towards 300, having left previous record-holders Phil Bennett and Don Clarke well behind. If any afternoon epitomised Irvine's style, it was the international against

France at Murrayfield in 1980. Scotland, with Irvine – way below his best – tailed 14-4, but with two tries from the full-back at his most devastating and outrageous, they scored 18 points in the last quarter to turn defeat into victory.

Peter Jackson

Peter Jackson was one of those mesmerising wingers who used guile as much as speed to

King John – one of the most exciting of a line of brilliant Welsh fly-halves, Barry John, gets in his kick before he can be challenged by Fergus Slattery of Ireland in the international of 1971.

Another brilliant fly-half kicks clear. This is Jackie Kyle, a generation earlier than Barry John, playing for Ireland against England in 1957.

destroy defences. He considered himself a better player as his career progressed because he thought that his feet used to move considerably faster than his brain, but eventually, when his feet slowed down, he was able to produce a better sense of co-ordination as he was catching up with himself. That sums up his modest attitude to his many talents – and there was no doubting he was a great favourite with crowds the world over. He won 20 caps for England and was one of the stars on the 1959 Lions' tour when he scored one of his two most famous tries. The other had come a year earlier in a bruising battle against the Australians which looked like ending in a 6-6 draw. England were a man short and when Jackson received the ball several minutes into injury time, the danger didn't look that obvious. But Jackson swerved and feinted round the wing and full-back to go over for one of Twickenham's legendary tries.

The Lions suffered badly at the boot of Don Clarke in 1959 and looked to retrieve some pride in the final Test. The Lions scored three tries to two New Zealand penalties, the visitors' first score being a Jackson special, as he left several defenders floundering in his wake. He finished his career by leading Warwickshire to a hat-trick of County Championship triumphs, that third triumph being his final match, as

Above *Willie John McBride in South Africa in 1974, when he crowned a long career, in which team success had come slowly, with a triumphant captaincy of the British Lions.*

Right *Lucien Mias catches a high loose ball. Mias was a great captain who finally disciplined the French into getting the results they deserved.*

he'd played all that season with a spinal disorder. But, as through his career, he left the crowd cheering a Jackson try.

Barry John

Wales seemed to produce a never-ending line of brilliant fly-halves. For many the greatest post-war exponent was Barry John, although Cliff Morgan, David Watkins and Phil Bennett all had their supporters. After the 1971 British Lions' tour to New Zealand, the Cardiff fly-half was christened 'King John', but he found the superstar status rather overwhelming, which resulted in him retiring after the 1972 international championship at the relatively early age of 27.

Although Barry John teamed up with Allan Lewis and Billy Hullin in his opening internationals, it was his partnership with Gareth Edwards that has gone into Welsh rugby legend. They linked up in 1967 against the All Blacks, but they were at their finest in 1971 when they helped Wales to their first Grand Slam since 1952 and then were at the heart of the Lions' triumph. The comment was made during that visit that it was a relief to see Barry John use the door to leave the room instead of just disappearing through the wall. By that tour John's reputation as a match-winner became complete when he added

Above *Andy Irvine, Scotland's exciting full-back, clearing to touch against England in 1982, ten years after his international début.*

Centre left *Nigel Starmer-Smith has the ball, but bearing down on him is the mighty form of one of rugby's all-time great players, New Zealander Colin Meads.*

Left *A most popular All Black captain, Graham Mourie led his country to their first Grand Slam in Britain in 1978.*

goal-kicking to his list of achievements. He passed a century of points in only eight games and finished with 189, a record for a tourist in New Zealand.

On his return the adulation he received made it difficult for him to lead a normal life and he soon retired, but not before he had set a then-record of 90 points for his country in his 25 appearances.

Cliff Jones

Although he retired at the very early age of 24, Cliff Jones was rated as the finest-ever to wear the No. 10 jersey for Wales. He'd been in the Welsh team for five seasons when he called it a day after the 1938 clash against Ireland. Jones captained Wales in his last season, but such was the pounding and rigours that fly-halves had to contend with in those days, that Jones felt he'd had enough. It was a shame because Cliff Jones on form was one of the most exciting sights on a rugby field – he was slippery as an eel, with electrifying pace able to split the most concentrated defence. He showed all the skills in only his second international, against Scotland in 1934, and soon became a great favourite with the crowd. One of his happiest moments came when Wales defeated the All Blacks by the odd point in 25 at Cardiff in December 1935. Jones remained involved in rugby and was president during Wales' centenary season in 1980-81.

Jackie Kyle

It says everything about the many skills of Irish fly-half Jackie Kyle that he was able to play international rugby for eleven seasons and still retain his effectiveness up till the very last. Kyle was a complete player – a brilliant runner and tactical kicker who also enjoyed the rough and tumble of defence. Flankers would have a job on their hands to keep him under wraps; if they relaxed for a second, he'd seize his chance and be away.

Kyle was known as 'The Ghost' in France, and after a fine tour with the 1950 British Lions in New Zealand, they nick-named him 'The Twins'. Kyle made his international début just after the Second World War, a period that brought several successes to Ireland. They won the championship in 1948, 1949 and 1951. The first

two were Triple Crown years and 1948 is also the occasion of Ireland's only Grand Slam. Around this time Ireland enjoyed some notable Triple Crown clashes with Wales, who have good reason to remember the magic of Jackie Kyle. By the time he retired in 1958, at the age of 32, he had played 46 times for Ireland, a world record at the time, plus another six Tests for the British Lions.

Willie John McBride

There can have been few more dedicated rugby players than Ireland's Willie John McBride. Because he had known depressing times on earlier tours, his reward for the great successes of the 1971 and 1974 British Lions was all the greater. He came into the Irish side in 1962, but despite being a stalwart of British rugby for the next 15 years, it was not until the 1970s dawned that he found the success he had been searching for.

Injuries on the 1971 Lions' tour meant he took over as pack leader a week before the first Test. His presence and inspiration not only helped bring the Lions that series, but ensured his selection for the 1974 tour to South Africa as captain. Earlier that year, he had led Ireland to their first success in the championship for 23 years. But South Africa was his finest hour. After his humiliations in 1962 and 1968, it gave him immense pleasure to bring Springbok rugby to its knees as the Lions gave their opponents the biggest hammering they've ever experienced. The sight of McBride being chaired off the field after victory in the third Test in Port Elizabeth said everything about their conclusive triumph.

McBride played one more season of international rugby to set a new world record of 63 Irish caps to go alongside his 17 Tests for the Lions. His last match resulted in a trouncing at the hands of the Welsh in Cardiff, but the game before, against the French, had the Lansdowne Road crowd cheering madly as he scored his first-ever try for Ireland.

Colin Meads

Colin Meads, the rugged New Zealand forward, is probably the outstanding rugby personality of all time. He was in the heart of New Zealand's scrum for 15 years and he epitomised the uncompromising, physical dedication of All Blacks' rugby. Meads was a talented forward, magnificent with the ball in his hands, a one-man symbol of rugby power. To some he was sometimes over-robust, and Meads was involved in several unsavoury incidents during his career – his sending-off in the international at Murrayfield against Scotland in 1967 being the most famous. But these should not detract his reputation as one of rugby's legends. Not only was he a great player, but he was a big enough man to change his ideas about power rugby and switch to the 15-man philosophies of Freddie Allen.

Although he filled in at flanker and No. 8 in his early days, it was in the All Black second-row that Meads was soon firmly embedded. Many felt that his best partner in the boilerhouse was his own brother, Stan, but family farm commitments meant a premature retirement for him. The All Black forwards of the 1960s formed a unit feared all over the rugby world – alongside Meads were Wilson Whineray, Ken Gray, Brian Lochore, Kel Tremain, Ian Kirkpatrick and Waka Nathan – and there were few sides which could come near to stopping or even containing them. Meads' final appearances came in the series against the 1971 Lions and it must have hurt him as All Black skipper to see New Zealand lose. But nothing could or can diminish from his tremendous service to rugby.

Lucian Mias

Lucien Mias is the man who managed to harness French flair so that they played to their capabilities and ensured that they became a consistent force in world rugby. Mias was a member of the French pack that were humiliated 25-3 by the Springboks in 1952, and it was a defeat that affected him badly. He knew that individually the French were as good as the South Africans, but they could not compete as a unit. That loss came in the first half of his career, as medical studies meant he had to give up after the 1954 championship. But Mias continued playing for his club Mazamet and, while losing three stone himself, made his club side into one of the most formidable units in France.

After a poor run, including the 1957 championship when they failed to score a single try, France asked Mias to lead them to South Africa in 1958. The result was

South Africa's first home defeat in a series that century and the following year France carried off the Five Nations title. Mias, after 25 caps, decided to call it a day again. He'd shown France the way to play together and his influence was to remain a long time after his departure.

Graham Mourie

New Zealand have a fine tradition for producing outstanding captains, none more so than flanker Graham Mourie who held All Black rugby together in the late 1970s and early 1980s. Because of South Africa's isolation and various celebrations, Europe, and Britain especially, was to see a lot of him. His consistency and level of performance was amazing and the All Blacks always seemed twice the team when he was in attendance. He first led New Zealand to France in late 1977, by which time he had formed a close relationship with coach Jack Gleeson. The pair were at the head of the All Blacks' first-ever Grand Slam in Britain in 1978, although sadly Gleeson was to die shortly afterwards. Mourie was to spend five successive winters in Europe, impressing everyone with his modesty and intuitive play. New Zealand remained undefeated in Tests in Britain, and the victory which must have given him the greatest pleasure was the 23-3 drubbing of Wales at Cardiff as part of the home side's centenary celebrations. The scoreline could have been double, and Mourie rounded off a fine display with a superb try which included a dummy more characteristic of a three-quarter.

George Nepia

Many rate the 1924-25 All Blacks as one of the greatest touring sides ever seen in Great Britain. And playing full-back for them was a 19-year-old Maori, George Nepia, who was to play in all the matches on that tour when the New Zealanders became known as 'The Invincibles'. That total of 30 matches says everything about his resilience, courage and stamina and by the end of the visit, many fans thought he was indestructible. The British were to see him at close quarters again on the 1930 Lions' tour, when they found him in the same sort of no-compromising form. Later, he turned to league and came over to this country to play rugby league in a short-lived experi-

Blond French flanker Jean-Pierre Rives catches the ball as the Welsh move in in the 1982 match. Rives was an inspiring French captain.

ment before returning back home. New Zealand rugby may be based around forward power, but Nepia will always be remembered as one of the great All Blacks.

Frik du Preez

South Africa has produced many powerful, ball-handling forwards and Frik du Preez was not only one of the fastest, but one of the finest. Some of his initial international appearances were made on the flank, but his agility in the line-out took him into the second row. He also occasionally kicked penalty goals for the Springboks.

In fact, his début came in Avril Malan's tour of Britain when he ended up as the second-highest scorer and firmly established in the South African scrummage, where he was to remain until 1972, by which time he had won 38 caps. A measure of the strength of Springbok rugby at the time can be seen in that he was on the losing side only eight times. It was during the first Test in the 1968 series against the British Lions that he scored one of the most famous tries in rugby as he peeled away from a line-out and raced 50 yards to score, powerfully outstripping a despairing Lions' defence. He finally teamed up with his adversary of old, Colin Meads, during the RFU centenary celebrations in 1971 – they enjoyed playing together almost as much as their many battles over the years.

Jean-Pierre Rives

France's Jean-Pierre Rives was the outstanding flanker produced by the northern hemisphere in the 1970s. His flowing blond hair made him instantly recognisable and helped show just how much ground he did cover during a game. In his early days, he formed part of a famous back-row unit with Jean-Claude Skrela and No. 8 Jean-Pierre Bastiat, but the other two retired before the end of the decade as Rives' assumed the captaincy of France. It was a difficult time for him; often the selectors did not agree with his attacking style and often did not help by chopping and changing his team. After winning the Grand Slam in 1981, France finished bottom in 1982 after breaking up the successful team of the season before.

Rives had burst upon the scene in 1975 and his wholehearted commitment soon won him many admirers. His attitude was that rugby was a game to be enjoyed and he was dedicated to an attacking style of game. Rives hated the 10-man game that many around him seemed to want, as he felt it would best suit France if they were allowed the freedom to express themselves. Sadly, that meant he spent as much time and energy battling away off the field as on it to prevent France from transferring to a negative style. For the future, that battle is as important as anything he has ever done.

Ken Scotland

In rugby today the sight of the full-back on the counter-attack, abandoning his full-back duties, is common enough, but that revolution only began in the late 1960s and 1970s. There's always someone ahead of his time, and in this case it was Scotland's Ken Scotland, a beautifully balanced runner, willing to attack and to go for tries without neglecting his full-back defensive requirements. He was a good kicker, and could punt superbly with either foot.

Right from his début game, when his six points brought Scotland a rare victory in Paris, Ken Scotland proved himself a player of true class and he was to remain a regular for the next eight seasons. It was in that hardest of rugby countries, New Zealand, with the British Lions in 1959, that his place among the rugby greats was confirmed. In his first match there, Scotland ran in three tries from the full-back spot against Hawkes Bay, the first of ten he was to score. He was good enough to play international rugby at centre and fly-half and he was a key figure in the legendary London Scottish side that dominated the Middlesex Sevens in the early 1960s. Scotland won the last of his 27 caps in the same place he had won his first – Paris – in 1965, by which time he had well and truly shown the way for the future full-back to follow.

Wavell Wakefield

Known simply as 'Wakers', Wavell Wakefield, later Lord Wakefield of Kendall, was the dominant figure in the first century of English rugby. His total of 31 caps was a record until 1967 and he was twice asked to lead the British Lions, in 1924 and 1930. Wakefield was a magnificent forward, who was the inspiration behind England's greatest era in the 1920s. He reorganised the England scrum and their record of achievement in this period is unparalleled – four Grand Slams (1921, 1923, 1924, 1928). Much of the credit must go to the influence of 'Wakers', and his service to rugby did not end with his playing career. He served on the international Board from 1954-61 after being president of the Rugby Football Union. Wakefield was a great servant of Harlequins, the RAF and Middlesex and he was to hold a seat in both the House of Commons and the House of Lords. Even into the 1980s, by which time he himself was also well into his eighties, he was still holding strong opinions on the game and the way it should be played. Just as in his playing days, he was determined to get things right.

J. P. R. Williams

Rugby's courage and commitment has never been more evident than in the play of

Left *Sotland of Scotland. One of the first of the modern attacking full-backs was British Lion Ken Sotland.*

Above *A courageous and tough rugby player, J. P. R. Williams running with the ball from full-back for Wales against the All Blacks.*

Rhys Williams gets the ball out from a maul to his scrum-half Evans when playing for Wales in 1958.

Wales' full-back John Williams, the sporting doctor who was simply known as 'JPR'. The change in the laws opened the way for the new style attacking full-back in the 1970s and there was no greater exponent of the new freedom than Williams. But while his spectacular forages upfield brought a new dimension to the game, it was his complete mastery of the defensive game which made him such an effective player.

His international career spanned three decades and by the close he had collected 55 caps, a Welsh record. He came into the side in 1969 along with Mervyn Davies, and their arrival heralded another golden era for Wales. Williams also toured twice with the British Lions – 1971 and 1974 – when they won both series, in New Zealand and South Africa. Back home, he was the pillar on which the challenges of the other countries in the Five Nations Championships often failed. Williams selected England for special treatment. His eleven outings were all victorious and he scored five tries, four of them at Twickenham. After leading Wales to a fourth successive Triple Crown in 1979, he retired, but returned in the centenary season to play three more times for his country and this took him past Gareth Edwards' total record of 53 caps.

An all-round sportsman, J. P. R. Williams hoped to set up a clinic specialising in sports injuries on his retirement.

Rhys Williams

Much of the spotlight in the years after the Second World War shone on the talented British three-quarters, but battling away among the forwards was a Welshman with the skill and capacity to compete with the best New Zealand and South Africa could offer. He was Rhys Williams, a lock who was tall in the line-out, strong in the maul and was once described by his skipper Clem Thomas: 'You never heard Rhys, but by God, you felt his presence.' Williams made his début for Wales in 1954, and it took him only until the following summer on the Lions' tour of South Africa to prove himself amongst the world's best. On the tour he was the backbone of the Lions' scrum as he was to be in New Zealand four years later. At the end of the visit, the five outstanding players in the Tests were selected and Rhys Williams was the only forward named. He was to play in only one more game for Wales – against England at Twickenham in 1960 – but, as skipper, his 23rd match and finale was not the occasion he hoped it would be. In dazzling début Richard Sharp inspired England to a 14-0 lead at half-time and Wales never recovered. Williams had served Wales and British rugby well, but unfortunately he was never to play in a Welsh Grand Slam or Triple Crown side – he had, at least, deserved that.

The Five Nations Championship

Mervyn Davies

The highlight of any domestic season, once the touring party has left our shores, is the Five Nations Championship. The celebration of winning the Grand Slam is anticipated, but the thought that the wooden spoon can be yours for a season is also there. In recent years, we have become used to the champions also completing the Grand Slam – Wales, France and England have all conquered the other four in a season in the past few years. The Scots and Irish have not been so lucky and must look back down the years to a single triumph – Scotland in 1925 and Ireland (who went close in 1982) in 1948.

I was lucky enough to be part of Wales' successful 1970s and our achievements in that decade have taken us ahead of England in Triple Crown victories and outright championships. But while winning four Triple Crowns in successive seasons in the 1970s, it was a sobering thought to recall that after Wales won the Triple Crown in 1911, they had a 39-year wait until the next one.

Every country can look back to a golden era (or in some cases, eras). For the English

the 1920s saw them at their peak, when the England scrum included Tommy Voyce, Bonnie Cove-Smith, the irrepressible 'Wakers' – Lord Wakefield of Kendall – and those guiding lights at half-back, Kershaw and Davies, who were undefeated in their 14 England internationals together. It had taken England until the 1920s to recover from the 'broken time' dispute which split rugby in that country in 1893. Since those heady days, England have only achieved two Grand Slams – 1957 and 1980 – and, in the 1970s especially, have given their long-suffering supporters a torrid time.

The 1970s, for Wales, was the second great era. The first had come in the opening decade of the century. Between 1900 and 1911, Wales lost only seven matches out of 43 and picked up six Triple Crowns. But Wales won only three championships between the Wars and, apart from a couple of successes at the beginning of the 1950s, it wasn't until the mid-1960s that they started disturbing the record books again. The emergence of world-class players like Gareth Edwards, Barry John,

England playing Wales at Blackheath in 1892 and apparently scoring a try under the posts. England won 17-0.

Ireland's captain in the Triple Crown winning year of 1982, Ciaran Fitzgerald, and colleague Moss Keane appear to be saying 'What's up, ref?' in the match with Scotland.

J. P. R. Williams of Wales tackled in the international against England in 1979. Williams always played his best and was most successful against England.

J. P. R. Williams, Gerald Davies and Phil Bennett along with a talented bunch of forwards meant that Wales enjoyed as much success in the 1970s as they did at the beginning of the 1900s.

Unfortunately for Scotland, their best period of rugby coincided with that first Welsh golden era, but they still picked up three Triple Crowns just after the turn of the century. Since the Second World War, their cupboard is bare as far as Triple Crown and Grand Slams go – nor have they won the championship outright. Often they've been one of the most attractive sides in the championship and been involved in some of the most exciting

matches. Twice in the 1970s, under the inspiring leadership of Ian McLauchlan, they travelled to Twickenham on the last leg of that long-awaited Triple Crown, only to be denied – the second time by a single point. They shocked the rugby world in the final match of the 1982 championship when they inflicted Wales' heaviest-ever home defeat and took away Wales' championship ground record that stretched all the way back to 1968.

That 1982 Championship also saw the rejuvenation of the Irish. They notched up their first Triple Crown since 1949, no mean achievement considering they'd been whitewashed the season before. The Irish, like the Scots, are short of that depth of talent which allows a sustained period of success, although helped by the skilful fly-half Jackie Kyle, they won three championships in four years after the Second World War. But, generally, again like the Scots, what they lack in ability they make up for in spirit, and both countries have always been difficult to beat on their own soil. Even when Wales and England have been at their peak, a victory at Lansdowne Road or Murrayfield was a triumph to treasure.

The French took some severe hammerings in their early days from the home countries, but, by the 1920s, they were giving as good as they got. But after accusations of payments to players, the French were left out in the cold from 1931 until after the Second World War. Their first championship came in 1959 but, being ineligible for the Triple Crown, they had to wait until 1968 for a Grand Slam. They were the only country to challenge Wales seriously in the past decade, and added two more Grand Slams in 1977 and 1981.

Although the opening encounter between England and Scotland took place at Raeburn Place in Edinburgh in 1871, it was not until 1883 that the International Championship came into force. Initially it was a Four Nations Championship because France did not join the others until 1910. Only four of the first seven championships were completed for various reasons, with England winning the first two outright and Scotland one. All the home countries won titles before the new century, but with England's talent reduced drastically by the 'broken time' dispute, when representatives from the Northern clubs proposed that 'Players be allowed compensation for bona-fide loss of time'. This split eventually led to the formation of Rugby League and seriously weakened England's attempts to dominate the Championship.

For Wales, one of the most significant matches was the last international ever

England playing Scotland in the drawn Calcutta Cup match in 1982. Scotland's Jim Renwick tackles England's Paul Dodge.

Alderson relieves the English line in the match against Scotland at Raeburn Place in 1892, won 5-0 by England.

One of Wales' great post-war fly-halves, Cliff Morgan, kicks into touch against France in 1956. On the right is Bryn Meredith.

played at Stradey Park, the home of Llanelli. The date was 11 March 1893 and, having defeated England by a single point and won up in Scotland, the Welsh were only one win away from their first-ever Triple Crown. It was the first full season that Wales had introduced the four three-quarter system and, although it was bringing results, there were still some teething problems. At the heart of the Welsh midfield was Arthur 'Monkey' Gould, the first Welsh superstar, and behind him at full-back was the legendary full-back Billy Bancroft. Gould was captain, but it was his co-centre and brother Bert who stole the glory in front of 20,000, as he scored the only try of the afternoon to see Wales home, 2-0 (the try was half the value it is today). The Welsh machine was rolling and getting ready to dominate the 1900s.

Ireland got their own back the following year when they defeated Wales by a penalty goal for their first Triple Crown. The game is known as the Ballinfeigh Bog match as it was played in terrible conditions; the narrow score-line did not reflect Ireland's domination.

The new century heralded a glut of Welsh rugby talent – Percy Bush, Dickie Owen, Rhys Gabe, Gwyn Nicholls and Billy Llewellyn. Although Wales' most important victory in this period was out-

A determined Irish run in the match against England at Richmond in 1898. Ireland won 9-6.

side the championship – inflicting the only defeat on Dave Gallaher's 1905 All Blacks – their continuing success was remarkable. In a 12-year period, Wales won six Triple Crowns and six outright titles.

The last of those titles was won at the Arms Park on 11 March 1911, when, as often happened then, Wales and Ireland met with both bidding for the Triple Crown. Wales had had an impressive season – four tries against England, eight against Scotland and three against France. Everyone wanted to see the final match and the gates had to be shut an hour before the kick-off. Unfortunately, those waiting outside weren't keen on missing the match and so they attacked the gates and forced their way in. Some clambered onto the roofs of the stand, only for a few to fall off. It was a gruelling forward battle, but the Welsh experience told and they eventually ran in three tries to win 16-0 and notch up their third Grand Slam.

Without quite as much fuss, Scotland were enjoying a successful period; between 1887 and 1907, they were involved in ten championships. It was the Scottish pack that formed the cornerstone of their triumphs, with Mark Morrison an outstanding captain on 15 occasions. The Scots' best season was 1906-07 when they defeated Carolin's Springboks as well as the other home countries. The hardest match was against the Welsh at Inverleith in Edinburgh. Wales had just reverted to their seven forwards-eight backs strategy to hammer the English, but that innovation

lost a lot of credibility when the Scots scored two tries to Bert Winfield's penalty goal. Up till that match, it looked as though the new formula might be accepted in the same way the three-quarter system had been. The years immediately preceding the First World War saw the emergence of England, who were beginning to recover from the split in their camp. One of their most significant matches was the very last international before the outbreak of hostilities. England had won a Grand Slam in 1913 and travelled to Inverleith a year later in search of another. The Scots had not won a game that season, but played a full part in a tremendously exciting game.

Michel Crauste of France receives a wet ball at Twickenham in 1961. Roberts moves in to tackle.

At one stage the Scots trailed 16-6, but fought back to within one point although the English held out to remain unbeaten. All the countries suffered badly through loss of life in the next four years – of those who played in that final Calcutta Cup, five English and six Scots were to be killed in action.

The years after the war were to be dominated by Scotland and England. The Scots had some magnificent running backs, but it was the English forwards who dominated the period. England won four Triple Crowns – 1921, 1923, 1924 and 1928 – and each time they also carried off the Grand Slam. The motivating force in the scrum was 'Wavers' Wakefield – he organised the back-row and gave England a solid scrummaging base. He led England on 13 occasions and was invited to captain the Lions in 1924 and 1930 (he was unavailable both times). England had won only once in Wales since 1895, but the record was put straight at Swansea in 1924. Two

years earlier, England had been thumped 28-6, but this time they turned the tables with tries by Cartson Catcheside (2), Eddie Myers, Herbert Jacob and Harold Locke. Interrupting this England success was Scotland's first, and as yet last, Grand Slam. The three-quarter line of Smith (the Flying Scot), Macpherson, Aitken and Wallace – all Oxford University men – was one of the finest units of all time, supported by the talented play of Dan Drysdale at full-back. The Scots had beaten France at Inverleith and then travelled away to defeat Wales and Ireland. The game against England on 21 March 1925 marked the opening of the Murrayfield ground. It looked as though it was going to be a disappointing day for the Scots as they trailed 5-11, but they fought back and near the end Herbert Waddell, now president of the Barbarians, dropped the goal that sent the Scottish banners high.

The economic depression in the 1920s seemed to affect the Welsh more than the other countries; and their record in that decade of only eight wins in 30 matches against England, Scotland and Ireland contrasted with their achievements just before the war. Although the 1930s did not bring much more material success, Wales did produce some magnificent players – Cliff Jones, Viv Jenkins, Wilf Wooller and a young schoolboy Haydn Tanner. Their most memorable match in this period was the 1933 clash against England at Twickenham. The Prince of Wales was among the 64,000 to see the Principality notch up their first-ever win at HQ. Jenkins and Wooller were making their débuts. Wales trailed 0-3 at the interval, but a try and dropped goal from Ronnie Boon saw Wales home, glad at last to have ended the Twickenham bogey at the tenth attempt. Scotland ended up champions, though, in 1933, and with France excluded, the title went to England, Ireland and Wales in the following years. England's 1934 triumph also brought a Triple Crown, and Ireland's championship in 1935 was their first for 36 years. Yet, they still found the Welsh a major stumbling block. Four times in the 1930s Ireland met Wales as the final obstacle in search of the Triple Crown and four times they failed. The most memorable match was the 1936 clash in Cardiff. The gates were closed two hours before the start, but local firemen had to be called to try and regain control as thousands broke in. Eventually, the match began with about 15,000 extra spectators inside, many drenched as the firemen had used their hoses to calm them down. There was plenty at stake for both sides. A win for Ireland would give them their first Triple Crown for 37 years and a victory for Wales would give them the

Above Scotland playing Ireland in 1979. Ireland smuggle the ball back from the maul.

Opposite top England playing Wales in 1982. Phil Blakeway gets the ball back despite the presence of several Welshmen, who are being fought off by Peter Winterbottom.

Opposite below Moss Keane of Ireland and Nigel Horton of England jump high at a line-out in the 1979 match.

championship. Wales had already seen off the challenge of the All Blacks and their hopes were high for another golden era, with that fly-half wizard Cliff Jones as a key figure. In the end a solitary first-half Viv Jenkins penalty goal separated the sides, although a dropped goal attempt by Victor Hewitt in the closing minutes nearly snatched victory – a dropped goal at that time was worth four points.

The last outright championship went to Scotland in 1938, even now the year of their last Triple Crown. The championship was clinched at Twickenham in what has become known as 'Wilson Shaw's match'. Twickenham has not exactly been a happy hunting ground for the Scots – that 1938 success is one of only three victories there – the others were in 1926 and 1971. The 1938 Calcutta Cup was watched by King George VI and Queen Elizabeth, who saw Scotland fly-half Wilson Shaw give a virtuoso performance, scoring two tries and creating a third as the Scots scored five tries to England's one, although the score-line was rather closer, 21-16. Shaw was chaired and cheered from the field on one of Scotland's most famous rugby afternoons. The Scots ended up with the wooden spoon the following season as they lost all three games and the title was shared by England, Ireland and Wales (Ireland beat England, England beat Wales and Wales beat Ireland to deny them the Triple Crown for the seventh time). Although Wales had produced many marvellous players in the 1930s the decade was not dominated by any country as England had ruled in the 1920s.

The years immediately after the Second World War found Wales and Ireland the strongest. With France back in the fold, the Grand Slam also became a possibility again, but Ireland were wary in 1948 when they entertained Wales at Ravenhill in Belfast, as they went for a first Grand Slam and a third Triple Crown – the last had been in 1899. But the Welsh had proved the stumbling block so often and their post-war team contained some famous names – Bleddyn Williams, Billy Cleaver, Haydn Tanner, Glyn Davies, and Ken Jones among the backs. Jackie Kyle made a try for Barney Mullan to open the scoring, but Wales drew level when Bleddyn Williams side-stepped his way through the Irish defence. Ireland's winning score came early in the second-half when London Irish prop Jack Daly chased a kick through from a line-out to score the try that gave Ireland the title. The jubilant crowd tore the jersey from his back and there are pieces of Jack Daly jersey in many households throughout Ireland – probably enough pieces to make 15 jerseys!

Ireland were on the Triple Crown trail again in 1949, but this time they had to travel to Swansea. Ireland were captained by Karl Mullen, a hooker, and backing up Kyle's considerable talents at fly-half was a formidable back-row of Jim McCarthy, Des O'Brien and Bill McKay. At Swansea it was Jim McCarthy who emerged the hero as the scorer of the only try of the game. The points came from a well-practised Irish move that had Kyle breaking towards the blind-side and then punting infield where the speedy McCarthy was waiting to touch-down. The Welsh claimed that he was off-side, but they couldn't persuade referee Tom Pearce of England, so Ireland had picked up a second successive Triple Crown. Ken Jones was the only non-Cardiff man among the Welsh backs, but try as they might they could not break down the Irish defence. At the end of the game, it was Jim McCarthy's turn to have the jersey ripped from his back as the Irish celebrated their first win at Swansea since 1889.

There was no way, however, that all this Welsh magic could be kept down for too long and in 1950 John Gwilliam's team carried off their first Triple Crown since 1911. Fittingly, Belfast was the scene of the final leg of their quest. The scores were level at 3-3 with just a few minutes

England hooker Peter Wheeler leaves a Frenchman on the ground as he comes away with the ball in the 1975 Five Nations Championship.

Left *A try for Gareth Edwards and Wales against England at a muddy Cardiff Arms Park in 1971. Wales won 22-6.*

Bottom *France won an exciting match 20-14 against Wales in Paris in 1967, and scored a try in the last minute. In this picture a French back runs round two Welshmen.*

Below *One of England's most exciting runners in recent years is left winger Mike Slemen, seen handing off Elgan Rees of Wales in 1979 while Alastair Hignell backs up.*

remaining. The Welsh disrupted an Irish heel in the home side's '25' and harrassed scrum-half Carroll and fly-half Kyle. The ball went via Billy Cleaver who raced in for Wales' winning score, despite the attentions of Irish defenders and his proximity to the touch-line. A fortnight later, Wales clinched their fourth Grand Slam with a comfortable win over the French at Cardiff.

Although Ireland won the championship the following year, they were again denied the Triple Crown by Wales who drew 3-3 in Cardiff. There were two players making their débuts in the Wales team that day; a second row from Newport called Ben Edwards who was not to play again for his country, despite kicking Wales' 3 points – the other an impish-faced young Cardiff fly-half called Cliff Morgan. Wales were on the Grand Slam and Triple Crown trail again in 1952, but the most significant match of that championship was the opening encounter against England at Twickenham. Wales had only won there twice before and when they trailed by six points with full-back Lewis Jones a virtual passenger on the wing, it seemed unlikely that they would return home victors. But just before half-time Cliff Morgan broke through to put Ken Jones over for a try which Malcolm Thomas converted to leave Wales one point adrift. Wales stole a famous victory when the hobbling Lewis Jones joined the attack to

England's famous pack of 1980 in control against France. Bill Beaumont is on the ground but Ruger Uttley and his colleagues have got the ball back and are preventing the French coming through.

make the extra man which gave Ken Jones the space for his second try. Wales went on to their second Grand Slam in three years.

The mid-1950s saw England make a return to the top. Among the forwards were the giant locks David Marques and John Currie, hooker Eric Evans, who played for England when he was 37, and the battling flanker Peter Robbins. Among the backs was brilliant Jeff Butterfield and that mesmerising magician Peter Jackson. Dickie Jeeps was soon to take a guiding hand at scrum-half to give England their best-balanced team since the 1920s. They were champions three times in six years, beginning in 1953, collected two Triple Crowns and won their first Grand Slam (1957) since the day of 'Wakers'.

Scotland were rather in the doldrums. They had amazed everyone by thrashing Wales 19-0 in the 'Murrayfield Massacre' – not a bad result against a team which had won the Grand Slam the season before and was going to win another in the next. But Wales seemed to have no real worries as they journeyed to Murrayfield in 1955; they'd already beaten England and the Scots had gone 17 matches without a draw, let alone a win. With Wales leading 3-0 at the interval, everything seemed to be going according to plan, but the form-book was turned upside down in the second-half, with débutant Arthur Smith scoring the try that turned the game Scotland's way

allowing them to run out eventual winners 14-8.

Wales then beat Ireland easily and had to travel to Colombes in Paris to try and prevent the French from winning the championship outright for the first time. Led by back-row forward Jean Prat, France had been in impressive form, but they could not cope with the fiery Welsh pack led by Rees Stephens and the visitors won 16-11. The French were very disappointed, but it was obvious to all observers that it would only be a matter of time before they gained a title.

Despite Wales winning the 1956 Championship, Ireland were very glad to deny them the Triple Crown at Dublin. Wales struggled the following year and for the first time since 1937 lost their opening two matches. England were the team in form. In the final match, they hosted Scotland at Twickenham, as they pressed for their first Grand Slam for 29 years. England were easily the better team on the day, but the Scots fought determinedly, trailing only 3-6 with a quarter of an hour to go. Eventually, England found a way through to score two more tries to gain the Calcutta Cup, the Championship, the Triple Crown and the Grand Slam. England were champions again in 1958, despite drawing with both Scotland and Wales. Their outstanding performance came in Paris when France went down 14-0. That was the

turning point for France; the captaincy went to Lucien Mias and, after a successful summer tour of South Africa, they returned for an assault on the 1959 championship. Despite drawing with England and losing to Ireland, France's victory over the Scots in the opening match meant that if they beat Wales the title was theirs for the first time after 49 seasons of playing against the home countries. The game was played in a heatwave, always the weather likely to bring out the best in the French. They were well on top at the end as the Welsh ran out of steam, and two tries from Francois Moncla saw them at the top of the table. Lucien Mias was chaired off the field on that historic day for France. The French were involved in the next three titles, twice winning outright and, in 1960, sharing the spoils with England. One of France's most conclusive displays was the 1962 clash against England in Paris. Star of France's 13-0 victory that afternoon was flanker Michel Crauste – known as the 'Mongol' or 'Attila' because of his almost ghostly complexion. Crauste scored a hat-trick of tries in France's 13-0 victory. France had high hopes of a Grand Slam as they had also seen off the challenge of Scotland and Ireland – all was set for the match against Wales in Cardiff on 24 March 1962. A Kelvin Coslett penalty goal left France frustrated again, and they were going to have to wait another six years for that

elusive Grand Slam. It was Wales' only win of the season, although they didn't play Ireland before November that year because of a smallpox outbreak in the Rhondda. Still, Wales went through the championship without scoring a try, and only managed three penalties.

England took the championship in 1963, but any sort of honour was to elude them for the next 17 years. That period was dominated by the French and, especially, the Welsh. Even now that 1963 campaign lingers in the minds of England's supporters, because it contains the last time that England travelled down to Cardiff and won. Led by fly-half Richard Sharp, who had bemused Wales on his début three years earlier, a new-style England XV made the most of their opportunities to win 13-6. Wales also introduced some changes, including the half-backs, scrum-half Clive Rowlands (who was also made captain on his début) and fly-half David Watkins. The most famous match of the 1963 championship was the Calcutta Clash at Twickenham when Richard Sharp scythed his way through the Scottish defence, threw a cheeky dummy to Scottish full-back Colin Blaikie and went over for the try that took England into the lead, after the Scots had been 8-0 in front. That was one of the 'great' tries, although the English would have savoured it even more if they had realised then how long they were going to

Ireland's captain, Fergus Slattery, using a certain amount of emphasis to get over a point to Stewart McKinney during an international at Twickenham.

have to wait before their side were to win a championship again.

Scotland shared the title with Wales in 1964, the only time they have been at the top of the table since the Second World War. But it was Wales who were really on the ascendancy. Under Clive Rowlands' leadership, they took their first Triple Crown for 13 years the following season. They then travelled to Paris with hopes also of a Grand Slam – they knew the championship was theirs whatever happened but, unbelievably, they found themselves trailing by 22 points. Wales recovered slightly with three tries, but the game was perhaps most memorable for referee Gilliland of Ireland bursting a blood vessel in his left calf. The outstanding moment came near the end of one of the most boring Calcutta Cup matches. Scotland, without a win, were leading 3-0 and looked to be heading for their first win at Twickenham since 1938. In the dying minutes, the Scots were on the attack, but the England centre Mike Weston recovered the ball and fed it to winger Andy Hancock near his own line. Only a madman would have tried to run with it, but that was what he did and he beat the initial cover.

Suddenly, the crowd were on their feet cheering and an exhausted Hancock slumped over the line. There were those who thought that he should have run round under the posts, but he'd done enough damage to Scotland's dreams without inflicting defeat. Don Rutherford missed the conversion and the teams finished level. For a second successive Twickenham Calcutta Cup, an Englishman had scored an amazing try to thwart Scottish hopes of a rare victory on English soil.

Wales were champions again in 1966, courtesy of one of the finest tries ever seen at the Arms Park. In the championship decider between Wales and France, it looked as if the visitors had won the day; they led 8-0 after only 12 minutes and with ten minutes remaining still led 8-6. With France on the attack, Jean Gachassin threw a long pass, but it was intercepted by Stuart Watkins who set off for the French line. It was no simple task; there were about 75 yards to go and Watkins had to beat off the tackle of French full-back Claude Lacaze. To a tumultuous ovation he reached the French line and crashed over for the try which allowed Wales to retain the championship for the first time in 57 years.

France were denied their Grand Slam a year later when Scotland won by a single point in Paris, but they still won the title. That 1967 championship saw the début of Barry John and Gareth Edwards, but the most remarkable performance came from an 18-year-old Newport centre who made his début in the game against England; his name was Keith Jarrett, and his 19 points marked an outstanding beginning to an international career. Jarrett was not accustomed to the full-back role – his trial there against Newbridge just before this match was a disaster and he was switched back to centre at half-time. But the Gods were smiling and everything went right. His first penalty attempt bounced off a post and went over; from then on it was plain sailing. The highlight of the afternoon came when England centre Colin McFadyean kicked open out of defence – Jarrett came running on to the bounce and kept running, right to the England try-line for the first Welsh full-back try since Viv Jenkins' effort against Ireland in 1934, 33 years earlier.

France put the record straight in 1968 with their first-ever Grand Slam, but the following year saw the development of the Welsh team that was to dominate the 1970s. Edwards and John were joined by J. P. R. Williams and Mervyn Davies; Gerald Davies was already on the scene. Only a draw in Paris denied them their first Grand Slam for 17 years. France and Wales shared the 1970 championship.

The 1971 Five Nations Championship was one of the best. Wales dominated, but were lucky to win at Murrayfield. The Scots were at their inspired best and the

Scotland against Wales in 1981, and David Leslie comes away with the ball for Scotland with Welshmen on either side of him.

lead changed hands six times in all. The Scots looked to have clinched matters with a Chris Rea try which took them 18-14 ahead – the conversion was relatively simple and those two points would have taken the Scots out of reach. Unfortunately, Peter Brown's conversion rebounded back off the post, giving Wales one last chance. Wales won a Scotland throw at a line-out near Scotland's line. The Welsh went on one last desperate sortie and the intrusion of J. P. R. Williams gave Gerald Davies the space to round Scottish full-back Ian Smith to score the try which reduced Scotland's lead to a single point. Everything hung on John Taylor's conversion from the far touch-line. Between the posts it went for what has been described as the 'greatest conversion since St. Paul', and Wales went home 19-18 victors. Wales won their twelfth Triple Crown against Ireland, but had a fearsome task to try and complete the Grand Slam in Paris. Many members of that Welsh side claim that their showing in Colombes was one of their best. The French threw everything at them – even Barry John broke a nose with a 'do-or-die' tackle on Benoit Dauga. The moment that signified Wales' resolve was when J. P. R. Williams intercepted a French pass near his own line when it looked as if the home side were sure to score. Most teams would have been happy just to clear the danger, but Williams charged up-field on the counter-attack. As he neared the French 25, he swerved infield to allow Gareth Edwards to support on the outside and the cheeky scrum-half was over for a try. Barry John, returning after treatment on his nose, floated through for a try in the second-half to seal the victory, but it was the Welsh defence which was the outstanding feature

of their triumph on that day.

A week earlier, the Scots and English were continuing their personal Calcutta Cup battle at Twickenham. Scottish memories had to stretch back to Shaw's match in 1938 for their last success at HQ. With eight minutes left, England led 15-8 and were on course to upset the Scottish invaders once again. Duncan Patterson reduced the deficit with a try and Chris Rea sent Scottish hearts beating with a try out to the left in the very last minute of the game. Everything now depended on the conversion. The taker, as in the Welsh match, was Peter Brown with his distinctive style, and his name became folklore as the disbelieving English watched the ball sail comprehensively over the bar for Scotland's 16-15 success. This outstanding championship was a fitting preview for the highly successful British Lions' tour of New Zealand, led by Welsh skipper John Dawes.

That heralded a golden era for Wales and also for the championship in the 1970s. The troubles in Ireland meant that the 1972 Championship was incomplete, while for the first time there was quintuple tie in 1973 with all the countries winning two matches. Ireland ended a wait of 23 years when they clinched the 1974 title. Both Wales and France lost on the last day when victory would have seen them home, so Ireland, who were sitting out as spectators, were jubilant.

Wales won the championship in 1975, despite losing to the Scots at Murrayfield, and the following year notched up another Grand Slam. That was clinched in spectacular style at Cardiff against the French, who were also looking for the Slam. For many, one particular highlight was the

Welsh scrum-half Terry Holmes gets the ball away from the scrum as his French opposite number Gerald Martinez makes a grab and Jean-Pierre Rives comes round the back, 1982.

Below The man of the 1982 Five Nations Championship, Ollie Campbell of Ireland, successfully kicks another penalty on his way to 21 points against Scotland.

barging of French wing Gourdon into touch by J. P. R. Williams when a visiting try looked a certainty.

France made amends the following year with only their second Grand Slam, while Wales earned a second successive Triple Crown. Wales were back on the Grand Slam trail in 1978, and made it four championships out of five and four successive Triple Crowns in a row in 1979.

England had had a disastrous time in the 1970s, but the 1980s heralded a new era when Bill Beaumont's men took the Grand Slam for the first time in 23 years. After a narrow victory over Wales in a depressing game which had seen Welsh flanker Paul Ringer sent off, England went to Murrayfield on the last leg. In a thrilling game, which included three tries from England right-winger John Carleton, England won 30-18 and had that rugby nation cheering again.

Wales' domination had ended with the decade as all the countries became of equal standard. France won the 1981 Grand Slam, but finished the following season at the bottom, along with Wales. Ireland were the Triple Crown heroes of 1982, their first such achievement since 1949, with the 48 points of Ollie Campbell being crucial. Wales' last great link with the golden era was erased in the final match of that year when Scotland became the first championship team to win in Cardiff for 14 years, with five thrilling tries in an amazing 34-18 victory.

The Overseas Sides

David Norrie

The All Blacks

The rugby men of New Zealand – the All Blacks – are the most feared in the world. For long periods they have dominated the world scene and they still continue to produce the toughest forwards in the game. Even when they are going through a barren spell, New Zealand are the hardest rugby nation to beat. Since the isolation of South Africa, the All Blacks have almost single-handedly assumed the role of travelling the globe as Southern Hemisphere rugby giants. New Zealand have been frequent visitors to the UK in recent years, yet it's nearly 30 years since one of the home countries beat them on British soil.

Another of New Zealand's characteristics is the ability to find a regular supply of quality captains. Invariably they are forwards – the area where the real strength of New Zealand rugby lies. Men like Dave Gallaher, Cliff Porter, Jack Manchester, Wilson Whineray, Brian Lochore, Colin Meads and Graham Mourie have earned respect as much from their ability as leaders as from their performances on the international field.

Rugby was introduced in New Zealand in the 1870s and the game quickly established itself as totally suited to their talents and temperament. A native side visited Britain in 1888, but it was the visit of Dave Gallaher's 1905 All Blacks that showed what a force they were and helped to transform the game in this country. The New Zealand scrum, with two men in the front-row, three in the second and two in the back, allowed skipper Gallaher to rove around free as an extra scrum-half. The All Blacks swept aside all opponents, including England, Scotland and Ireland. But the game that is still talked about was the clash with Wales. The simple fact is that Wales won 3-0, but controversy has reigned ever since. The dispute concerns a try which All Black Bob Deans claims to have scored. By the time the referee arrived, Deans protested that he'd been hauled back by the Welsh defenders. The try was denied, but it sparked an intense rivalry between the two countries that has remained ever since. That loss was the only setback New Zealand had on their tour of Britain – they also thrashed France – winning 32 games out of 33, scoring over 800 points, 246 of them going to Billy Wallace. While Wales and New Zealand have fierce rivalry, the series between New Zealand and South Africa have produced some of the hardest international matches ever played. The two countries commenced hostilities in 1921 when New Zealand were the hosts and the Springbok tourists only lost two matches. With a win apiece and a draw in the third Test, the two shared that first series. The opening international at Dunedin was the scene of one of the most famous tries ever scored when New Zealand wing Jack Steele ran in a try from near his own line. That's happened before, but what made this all the more memorable was the fact he ran the length of the field with the ball clasped to his back. The initial pass went behind him and there was no time to adjust his grip.

The All Blacks returned to Britain in 1924 and Cliff Porter's men went one better and won all of their 30 matches, including two in France. Ever since, they've been simply known as the 'Invincibles'. The player best remembered from that visit was a 19-year-old Maori, George Nepia, who played in every match. Some rate him the finest full-back ever, and his record was a remarkable tribute to his resilience, courage and ability. There was no repeat of the close contest against Wales this time as the visitors triumphed 19-0. Their victory over England was soured when All Black Cyril Brownlie became the first international player ever to be sent off. His crime seemed

The first New Zealand match in the British Isles. The Maori team playing the Surrey Club at Richmond on 3 October, 1888.

The Two Umpires.

The 'Surrey Team' cheering the 'Maories' on their appearance

Their War Cry before starting Play.

The first Goal for New Zealand

A sudden outburst of Joy on getting the 1st Goal of the Tour.

Mobbed. 3 Cheers for the visitors. Hip Hip etc. etc.

Opposite top The Lions playing in Auckland, New Zealand, in 1959. Bev Risman dives over to score the winning try in the final Test, Don Clarke's tackle being too late.

Opposite centre South Africa beat the All Blacks 8-3 in the final Test at Port Elizabeth in 1960, to win the series. Hennie Van Zyl kicking when challenged by Watts.

Opposite below All Black Kevin Briscoe diving full-length to make a pass in a 30-3 victory over Border in South Africa in 1960.

all the more severe because his dismissal came within the hallowed grounds of Twickenham. New Zealand were not able to claim a Grand Slam because they did not play the Scots, who declined due to a dispute concerning the previous tour. That is a refusal the Scots now regret because they had a magnificent side in 1925, the year of their only Grand Slam.

The All Black-Springbok confrontation continued in 1928, but again the series ended in deadlock with two wins each. The All Blacks might have won had they been allowed to bring George Nepia, but South Africa's apartheid laws excluded him; it's difficult to imagine any touring teams travelling under such restrictions today.

The Lions toured New Zealand in 1930 and surprised the New Zealanders by winning the first Test. At the time, the Lions wore blue jerseys which meant the All Blacks became the All Whites for this series; the problem was solved after the Second World War when the Lions changed to scarlet, although the All Blacks went back to white in 1975 when the Scots toured there. The All Blacks won that 1930 series by winning the last three Tests, although it was the last season for many of the 'Invincible' side.

It was at this time that New Zealand finally decided to abandon their seven-man scrum and reintroduce the three-man front-row, but the 1930s were not a period of great success for them. On the 1935-36 British tour, they lost the Welsh and English internationals and were also beaten by Swansea at St Helens. A Russian Prince, Obolensky, was the two-try hero of England's 13-0 win, with his try two minutes before the interval rightly acknowledged as one of the great moments in rugby. Worse was to follow in 1937 when they lost the home series with South Africa. The teams went into the third Test level and the match was billed as the final decider as to who were the true world champions. South Africa won fairly comfortably, and because of the Second World War it was to be more than a decade before New Zealand could knock them off their top spot again.

The 1949 New Zealand tourists to South Africa suffered the ignomy of losing all four matches. The New Zealanders restored some pride by beating the 1950 Lions, but lost to Wales for the third time in four matches and Cardiff also recorded an historic victory. The crunch came in the 1956 series against the visiting Springboks. South Africa were on top of the rugby world and New Zealand wanted revenge for 1937 and 1949. The teams were level with two Tests to play when the All Blacks introduced a 16-stone 22-year-old full-back from Waikato called Don Clarke. His two penalty goals and conversion helped the All Blacks to a 17-10 victory and he was to dominate the rugby scene with his boot for the next eight seasons. Clarke's kicking clinched the series in the fourth Test and signalled the start of a golden era for New Zealand.

Clarke was at the centre of controversy when the British Lions came to visit in 1959. The Lions were a talented bunch, including the likes of Peter Jackson, Tony O'Reilly, Ken Scotland, David Hewitt and Bev Risman. The Lions' three-quarters were in sparkling form in the opening Test at Dunedin. They ran in four tries, but lost 17-18 with all those New Zealand points coming from the boot of Clarke with six penalty goals. The arguments continued for a long time about whether a kicker should be able to have such an influence on a match and should the value of the penalty goal be reduced. Clarke's talents finished

the Lions off in the second Test, this time with a last-minute try and conversion. New Zealand tied up the series in the third Test, but the Lions received some consolation when three fine tries ensured victory in the fourth. Ironically, the All Blacks could have saved the game near the end, but for once Clarke's penalty aim was off.

New Zealand and South Africa were in the thick of a tough struggle again in 1960, with the Springboks' home advantage proving the decisive factor. Prop Wilson Whineray was now leading the side and other members of his pack included Colin Meads, Ian Clarke (Don's brother) and Kel Tremain. That All Black side reached a peak in the mid-1960s when it steam-rollered its way over all the other major rugby-playing countries. France were defeated in three Tests in 1961 as were regular opponents Australia in 1962. England toured in 1963 and, although fairly easily defeated in the first international, put up a stern fight in the second and were only finally overcome by a 65-yard kick from Don Clarke after a mark. By now Ken Gray and Brian Lochore, as well as Colin Meads' brother Stan, were a vital part of a scrum that was feared the world over.

Only a scoreless draw against the Scots denied the All Blacks their long-awaited Grand Slam on the tour of Britain in 1963-64, when again Don Clarke's kicking was a crucial factor, although for the first time in his career he suffered a mid-tour loss of form. Including France, the All Blacks only suffered one defeat, a memorable day at Newport, in 34 matches.

Wilson Whineray's last series as captain came in the 1965 matches against South Africa. The All Blacks suffered a rare defeat in the third Test when the Springboks triumphed 19-16 after trailing 5-16 at the interval. Whineray's 30th game as captain in the fourth Test ended in victory. His record was impressive – 22 of those matches were won. Between that fourth Test defeat in South Africa in 1960 until that loss in the third Test in 1965, New Zealand were undefeated in international rugby, winning 15 of those 17 matches. Brian Lochore took over as skipper and led the All Blacks to a resounding 4-0 thumping of the 1966 British Lions. Lochore had Waka Nathan and Tremain beside him in the back-row, with the Meads brothers in the lock positions. Ken Gray, Bruce McLeod and Jack Hazlett formed the front-row. Most

were on the 1967 tour of Britain, when England, Wales, Scotland and France were beaten, but the All Blacks were denied the Grand Slam because the foot-and-mouth epidemic prevented the trip to Ireland. Chris Laidlaw and Earl Kirton were controlling affairs at half-back – both had been in Britain on Whineray's tour – but Laidlaw was being pressed by his understudy, Sid Going, who was to be a major influence on All Blacks' rugby for the next decade. Another flanker, Ian Kirkpatrick, also started making his name at this time. The major incident of the 1967 tour was the sending-off at Murrayfield of Colin Meads by referee Kevin Kelleher. Meads had been involved in several controversial incidents in his career, but many were surprised when his lunging at Scotland fly-half David Chisholm with his boot

earned the ultimate sentence. Many felt that his past had finally caught up with him, but his departure put a damper on New Zealand's victory that afternoon. France visited New Zealand in 1968 and Wales came the following year; France were beaten and Wales were hammered. Wales had travelled out as Five Nations Champions but they were defeated 19-0 and 33-12, with full-back Fergie McCormick claiming 24 points for the All Blacks in the second match.

The golden era was coming to an end. South Africa won the home series in 1970 and the 1971 British Lions blazed a trail through New Zealand to win two Tests, the first home series New Zealand had lost since the visit of the 1937 Springboks. Meads captained New Zealand in that series, but there were few of the old guard

Sid Going of New Zealand tackles Brynmor Williams of the British Lions in the second Test in New Zealand, 1977.

Opposite top *The All Blacks just beat Ireland 6-5 in Dublin in 1963, their superiority coming mainly from the line-out.*

Opposite centre *Chris Laidlaw, one of the best post-war All Blacks, kicking against England, 1967.*

Opposite below *Wilson Whineray, a great All Black captain, forcing his way through the French, 1964.*

left. And even Meads was missing when the 1972-73 All Blacks visited Britain under the leadership of Ian Kirkpatrick. It was an unhappy, surly tour, which culminated in New Zealand prop Keith Murdoch being sent home after an affray at the Angel Hotel, Cardiff, after New Zealand's narrow 19-16 win over Wales. By the end of the tour, although the All Blacks won three of the internationals and drew with Ireland, they'd been beaten four times – by Llanelli, the North-West Counties and the English Midland Counties West; the final defeat came in the last match, against the Barbarians in Cardiff, when the finest running talent British rugby could muster was unleashed with dazzling effects; the All Blacks responded to the challenge and played the best, unrestrained rugby of their tour, but there was no doubting that relationships had been severely strained on the visit.

The All Blacks then travelled to France where they lost the Test and in September of 1973 suffered a rare home defeat by touring England, an amazing result considering the English had lost three provincial games in the run-in to the Test. The great New Zealand side of the 1960s was gone for ever, and also badly missed was the coaching influence of Freddie Allen who had made a tremendous impact on world rugby.

The All Blacks made a successful visit to Ireland in 1974 as part of the home Union centenary celebrations. In the final week of the tour, they defeated Ireland, a Welsh XV and then drew with the Barbarians, who were fielding the 1974 Lions' pack. The All Blacks were led by No. 8 Andy Leslie and he also captained New Zealand to home victories over Scotland (24-0 in 1975 in the 'water polo' Test) and Ireland (11-3 in 1976).

Later that year, the All Blacks renewed rivalry with the Springboks in South Africa. But, despite winning the second Test, New Zealand went down in the other three and, as yet, have still to win a Test series on their chief rivals own soil. Hooker Tane Norton was skipper when the All Blacks beat the 1977 British Lions, who more than matched the New Zealanders' forward power, but were let down by sadly uninspired three-quarters.

New Zealand's revival continued later that year under coach Jack Gleeson and new skipper Graham Mourie on a tour of

France. After losing the first Test, the All Blacks gave warning of their return to form with a conclusive 15-3 victory in the second of the two internationals. The tourists were still rebuilding their scrum, but were producing some talented backs. The veteran Bryan Williams was still around, although the firebrand winger Grant Batty had to retire in 1977. Bruce Robertson was joined in the midfield by Mark Taylor and Bill Osborne, while Stu Wilson was a wing three-quarter of blistering pace and rare footballing ability.

New Zealand's long-awaited British Grand Slam came in 1978, when they clinched victory at Murrayfield. Earlier in the visit Munster had become the first Irish side to beat the All Blacks on an emotional afternoon at Thomond Park. Scotland and England had another chance to collect the All Black scalp the following year, but Mourie's side triumphed again, although they suffered their most comprehensive defeat ever on British soil when they were trounced 21-9 by the North of England at Otley. That success was not enough to carry England to victory a week later and they went down by a single point.

The All Blacks returned to Britain for a third year in a row as part of the Welsh Rugby Union's centenary celebrations. Wales were desperate to redress the balance which has been heavily in New Zealand's favour in the past quarter of a century. Wales had gone down to their old enemies in 1963, 1967, 1969 (2), 1972, 1974

Opposite top *The All Blacks playing the Barbarians in 1967 and Kel Tremain about to make a tackle.*

Opposite centre *Ken Gray goes for the ball for the All Blacks in a line-out against Wales in 1967.*

Opposite below *Gary Knights just gets over for an All Black try despite the grip Serfontein seems to have and the dive of Moolman (No. 5), New Zealand v South Africa, 1981.*

Ireland against New Zealand in 1978. Colin Patterson of Ireland wrestles the ball away while Mouric (left) is ready to pounce.

(an unofficial match) and 1976 – and 1980 was no different as Wales went under 3-23. Lock Andy Haden was a crucial influence at the line-out and the scavenging back-row of Mourie, No. 8 Murray Mexted and Mark Shaw tormented the Welsh at every opportunity. Amid great controversy, South Africa returned to New Zealand for the first time for 16 years in 1981. The tour, because of South Africa's apartheid laws, split New Zealand and caused civil disorder the like of which had never been seen before. The actual Test series was a fairly torrid affair as well, with New Zealand's full-back Alan Hewson deciding matters with the very last kick of the three-match internationals. The All Blacks were without Graham Mourie for these games because he had decided that he did not want to compete with South Africa. But he returned to France for what many reckoned would be his last major tour of Europe. He was at his best form and New Zealand won both the internationals. They could not claim to be world champions, though, because Australia had beaten them during the summer.

By the early 1980s, New Zealand had rediscovered their forward power, although it is unlikely they'll be back in Britain for a while; three tours in three seasons (five in five if you include France) was too many, and because of the fre-

quency of their visits, the All Blacks were beginning to lose their attraction. That would never do; they have played some of the finest rugby ever seen in Britain and brought some of the most famous touring sides. For most rugby players north of the equator there is no stiffer test in the sport than facing New Zealand, no matter how many times they come.

The Springboks

The political problems of South Africa have rather overshadowed their reputation as the toughest of rugby opponents, considered so by the Northern Hemisphere and the All Blacks alike. Until the all-conquering 1974 tour by the British Lions, the Springboks were undefeated in a major Test series at home this century, despite repeated attempts by Lions and New Zealanders alike. And until the tempestuous and troublesome visit to Britain by Dawie de Villiers' South Africans, their Test record on full tours to the UK was remarkable. After losing to Scotland on their first tour in 1906-07, they then completed four Grand Slams in a row – 1912-13, 1931-32, 1951-52 and 1960-61. De Villiers' side did not win a Test on their 1969-70 visit, but that was undoubtedly due as much to the off-the-field pressures as to a decline in their standard. The follow-

ing summer they again saw off the challenge of the All Blacks, who have yet to win a series on South African soil and have won only five internationals out of 20 on their visits there. The South African climate and conditions have produced forwards more used to the ball in their hands than their New Zealand counterparts where the grounds are heavier. The hard pitches, too, seemed to have bred powerful three-quarters, maybe not as agile as some of the touring Lions have been, but strong and determined runners as equipped for defence as they are for attack. Most of the legendary Springboks belonged to the middle five – the back-row and the half-backs – names like Bennie Osler, Danie Craven, Hennie Muller, Frik Du Preez, Doug Hopwood, Piet Greyling, Jan Ellis, Tommy Bedford, Dawie De Villiers and Morne du Plessis.

Rugby was brought to South Africa by British soldiers stationed in and around Cape Town in 1875 and the game spread so quickly that the South African Rugby Board was set up 14 years later. They weren't quite ready for the big time yet, because a British team, led by W. E. McLagan, went unchecked through South Africa two years later, winning all 19 matches including the three Tests. By 1896, the South Africans managed to win one international, and by the time the British

Piet Greyling touches down for the Springbok try against Ireland in 1970. The match was drawn 8-8.

came touring in 1903, they were more than ready. The first two Tests were drawn and South Africa won the third 8-0. In general, it was a hard tour with the British side only winning half of its 22 matches. These victories gave the Springboks the courage to tour Britain, a task made all the more difficult by the fact that they were following, only a season later, in the footsteps of Dave Gallaher's All Blacks. By the time Paul Roos' men left these shores, the rugby public were divided about which was the greater team. The South Africans had won their first 15 matches, but eventually went down to Scotland and Cardiff. More importantly, though, they collected the scalp that the All Blacks left behind, that of Wales, a nation who still to this day have not tasted the spoils of a victory over South Africa. The Springboks were firmly on the rugby world map now. This was emphasised before the First World War when they entertained the 1910 Lions and won the deciding third Test 21-5. The Springboks came back to Britain two years later when, despite losing to Swansea and Newport, as well as London Counties, they swept aside the four home countries, plus France, the closest contest coming in the 3-0 victory over Wales. The War postponed the clash of rugby giants that everybody was waiting for – the All Blacks against the Springboks. But that first series answered no questions because it was drawn, two Tests apiece,

with the fact that the South Africans were the visitors maybe giving them a narrow moral victory. The 1924 series, against the British Lions, marked the emergence of Bennie Osler – the 'evil genius' was his tag – and he was to dominate South African rugby for a decade. His prodigious kicking boot from fly-half was not loved by all, but they could not question its effectiveness. The Lions drew the third Test, but were well beaten in the rest, so after the All Blacks' successful 1924-25 tour of Britain, the All Blacks tour of South Africa in 1928 was eagerly awaited. Again, the series proved inconclusive, with New Zealand winning the fourth Test 11-5 to square the series. By South Africa's 1931-32 tour of Britain, Osler was partnered at half-back by a man who, even today, is still the voice of South African rugby, Dr Danie Craven. Although Craven finished playing at the age of 27, his rugby skills had allowed him time to represent the Springboks at scrum-half, fly-half, centre and No. 8. Osler was skipper on the British tour and they only lost one of their 26 matches, again winning all four Tests, a feat which took the All Blacks until 1978 to achieve. The most memorable moment came during the international against England at Twickenham when Gerry Brand dropped a goal for the Springboks from his own '25'. It was estimated that the ball travelled over 90 yards.

South Africa had a bad time against the British Lions in 1974, just avoiding losing every match. Lions captain Willie John McBride during the Test match at Ellis Park.

The Australians came to South Africa in 1933 for the first meeting between the two countries; the Springboks found them tough tourists and had to win the fifth Test to clinch the series. South Africa proved themselves the top rugby nation by beating the All Blacks on their own territory in 1937 and then defeating the 1938 British Lions. It was the power of the Springbok scrum which finally crushed the All Blacks in the crucial third Test. In all, the South Africans played 26 matches in Australia and New Zealand, winning five of the six internationals, only losing the second Test against New Zealand and the match against New South Wales. Their position was merely confirmed when Sam Walker's Lions lost the opening two Tests in a three-Test series.

South Africa, like all the other major rugby-playing nations, suffered with a loss of life during the Second World War, but seemed to recover quickest of the lot. The touring All Blacks were whitewashed in the 1949 series in South Africa, a humiliating experience for Freddie Allen's side. And the Springboks did their reputation no harm with an all but invincible tour of Great Britain during the winter of 1950-51 when they again completed the Grand Slam, losing only to London Counties in their 31-match visit. The outstanding result came in the international against Scotland at Murrayfield when the home side tumbled to a 44-0 defeat (lucky to get nothing) – the heaviest loss ever suffered in international rugby. Strangely, it was British rugby that flourished in South African conditions in the summer of 1955 when some of the finest three-quarter talent ever assembled from these shores took on the forward might of the Springboks. The first Test, in Johannesburg, is reckoned by many to be the finest international ever played, with the result hinging on the final conversion by Van der Schyff as the Springboks had hauled themselves back to within a point after trailing 23-11. That final kick drifted wide and the Lions were one up in the series. In the final analysis, the South Africans drew the series, 2-2, but their period of domination was coming to an end. The All Blacks exacted revenge for 1937 and 1949 in 1956, mainly through the emergence of goal-kicking Don Clarke, but the Springboks didn't have to wait long for a return visit.

Avril Malan captained the Springboks from lock and he had some impressive forwards around – Doug Hopwood at No. 8, Johann Claassen with him in the second row and the formidable scrummager Piet du Toit. Behind the scrum Keith Oxlee directed operations from fly-half and had the powerful John Gainsford beside him in the centre. With the great All Black pack of the 1960s coming together, it was a gruelling series for the forwards and

no place for the faint-hearted. With each side winning a Test and the third international drawn, it took a tremendous effort by the Springbok pack in the fourth to finally subdue the tourists 8-3. This form was continued on the tour of Britain that winter when they collected a fourth successive Grand Slam with their only defeat coming in the final traditional game against the Barbarians. The Lions were well beaten in the 1962 series, but the South African bubble finally burst in 1965. Malan's side lost the two internationals, to Scotland and Ireland, on a short tour of Britain. Then the Wallabies, who fought magnificently to draw a four-match series in South Africa in 1963, won the two home Tests against the Springboks. And in New Zealand, despite a tremendous fight back in the third Test, the tourists lost the three other Tests to the All Blacks. It was around this time that South Africa's political position became unacceptable to many and, as well as restricting their touring, it was to affect the standard of their rugby. The 1969-70 tour to Britain under scrum-half Dawie de Villiers was a succession of demonstrations, bad-tempered clashes and, not unsurprisingly, the Springbok rugby lacked the usual forward domination, despite the presence of Jan Ellis, Piet Greyling and Frik Du Preez. They were beaten by Scotland (for the third time) and England, although Ireland and Wales could only manage a draw. It was particularly upsetting for the Welsh because after six matches they have yet to lower the Springboks' colours.

Back home, the South Africans felt more secure and able to demonstrate their true worth, frustrating the All Blacks yet again in 1970, after crushing the Australians 4-0 in the series the summer before, but the day of reckoning was approaching. The Springboks got warning on the England tour of 1972 – Scotland, Wales and Ireland had all visited South Africa in the 1960s and had been well beaten. Yet, England, after being whitewashed in the International Championship earlier that year, went through South Africa unbeaten and defeated the Springboks in the Test. Worse was to follow with the visit of Willie John McBride's Lions in 1974. His side swept through South Africa, inflicting the Springboks' first defeat in a series at home during the century. The Lions' victories were conclusive proof that South African rugby had sunk to a depth never before experienced by that proud rugby country.

Under the leadership of No. 8, Morne du Plessis, they repaired some damage when the All Blacks failed in their quest on Springbok soil in 1976, but more and more the South Africans were having to rely on their own Currie Cup competition and visits from representative XVs for competitive rugby. The Lions toured in 1980 under Bill Beaumont, but, despite assuming the forward domination as in 1974, indecisive defence and inconsistent goal-kicking allowed South Africa to reverse that humiliating defeat. Although South African rugby was not as isolated as their cricket, touring abroad became a rarity. The 1981 tour of New Zealand was fraught with problems and split that nation as nothing had before. New Zealand won the three-match series with the final kick, but several games had to be cancelled and New Zealand will count the cost for years to come. At the moment, South Africa still entertain club and county sides, but it's possible that we will never again see Springbok rugby as we've come to know it.

The Wallabies

Rugby in Australia began in the Sydney area around the 1860s and 1870s, and it was the Southern Union that governed Australia's rugby affairs until the formation of the Australian RU in 1949. The sunny climate and hard grounds quickly established Australia's rugby reputation for a fast, attacking running style. They

Opposite top Jan Ellis of the Springboks challenged by Lions Phil Bennett, Fergus Slattery and Gareth Edwards in 1974.

Opposite bottom The Lions in South Africa in 1980. Lions captain Billy Beaumont high above the rest in the fourth Test.

Above When the Springboks toured New Zealand in 1981, there were the biggest and most sustained demonstrations against South African politics, and riot police were necessary at all the grounds.

Left Wallaby scrumhalf Des Connor gets the ball back to his three-quarters at Cardiff in 1958 despite the attentions of Barbarian John Faull.

The Lions at Sydney in 1959. Dickie Jeeps races away from a scrum as Wallaby half Des Connor tries to hold him. Syd Millar protects Jeeps from the pack.

entertained British teams in 1888 and in 1899, when they won their first-ever international 13-3 against a British Isles side.

They were still developing and it wasn't until 1908 that they felt strong enough to tour Britain. But by the time they made the tour, they'd been weakened by the 'professional' split which had affected English rugby 15 years earlier. With many key players defecting to the newly-formed rugby league, the party that came to Britain was not really reflective of the progress Australia had made. In the end they lost only five matches out of 31, beating England and losing narrowly to Wales in the two internationals. But any optimism for the future was cut short when 13 of the side turned to league on their return.

Things didn't improve after the First World War either, and the national side turned down an invitation to return as they didn't feel able to undertake a tour of Britain. But the invitation was taken up by

The Australians playing the Barbarians at Cardiff in 1958. Ron Harvey about to push the Baa-Baas's centre Phillips into touch.

John Hipwell, the Wallabies scrum-half, gets the ball away against Wales in Cardiff in 1973. Hipwell also toured in 1966-67, 1975-76, and 1981-82.

New South Wales – the 'Waratahs' – who became popular and successful tourists. Led by A. C. Wallace, who earlier had been a Scottish international, they beat Ireland, Wales and France, losing narrowly to Scotland and England. With their fast, attacking style, this party did a lot to repair Australia's image in the rugby world. And this was boosted to unparalleled heights, two summers later when they defeated the All Blacks 3-0 in a home series. Australian rugby continued on this high note when Australia travelled to South Africa to meet the mighty Springboks. The visitors shocked South Africa by winning the second Test 21-6, their speed around the park exposing the big and cumbersome South Africans. The home side recovered to win the next two Tests, but Australia had the last word when they won the fifth international 15-4. On returning home, Australia won the Bledisloe Cup for the first time, given by the then-Governor General of New Zealand for the winner of Wallaby–All Blacks contests. An Australian party actually arrived in Britain to tour, but when war was declared they returned home without playing a game. But the Wallabies came again just after the war in 1947-48 and again surprised British rugby. They lost only six matches out of 35 and beat Scotland, Ireland and England. One of the characters of that tour was Nick

Shehadie, later Sir Nicholas, who returned to manage the 1981-82 Wallabies to Great Britain. It was on the 1947-48 tour that the Barbarians began their tradition of playing the last game against the tourists. The Australians wanted to tour the United States and Canada on their way home and the Baa-baas agreed to play them to help provide them with funds. Thus began a tradition that has been maintained against touring sides ever since, although heavy snow cancelled the fixture in January 1982.

Greg Cornelsen, of the Wallabies, making a charge against Wales during the 1975-76 tour.

Australia playing Scotland in 1975, and John Hipwell in action.

Shehadie was in the side when the All Blacks were beaten in 1949 and later came back on the 1957-58 tour to Britain. Earlier, in 1953, the Wallabies had again surprised the South Africans by winning the first Test, although they lost the series. That tour of Britain was not very successful, but they will always be remembered for the Test against England when the Wallabies fell to an injury-time try in what is simply known after the scorer as 'Peter Jackson's match'.

That tour threw up the 19-year-old Jim Leneham as a full-back of undoubted class, and he was soon joined by the talented Ken Catchpole, for many the outstanding postwar scrum-half. He teamed up with fly-half Phil Hawthorne, which signalled the beginning of a successful era for the Wallabies. Led by John Thornett, they again rocked the Springboks in 1963 by winning the second and third Tests to eventually share the series. They had a mediocre tour of Britain in 1966-67, but collected the two scalps they prized most – Wales and England, although Ireland and Scotland, to whom they lost, repeated their victories when the Australians played two Tests on a short visit the following year.

But the great side was breaking up – Hawthorne went to rugby league and when Colin Meads tried to yank Catchpole out of a ruck with one of his legs trapped,

the great scrum-half's career came to a premature end. South Africa, who'd been beaten in a two-match series in Australia in 1965, gained their revenge in 1969 and 1971. The home countries all toured Australia in the late 1960s and 1970s, where Ireland were the sole victors. The England and Wales' tours caused much controversy, with the England prop Mike Burton being sent off in the second Test in 1975 and Graham Price, the Welsh prop, leaving the field with a broken jaw in 1978. Coach of Australia was former fiery forward Dave Brockhoff when England came to visit. The performance of his side's forwards in the opening minutes of that second Test was a shocking example of premeditated 'roughing up' and many believed that the coach was responsible for Australia's behaviour.

There was little sign of this animosity on their tours of Britain in 1975-76 and 1981-82, when the only Tests they won were the Irish ones. One of the mainstays of these sides was scrum-half John Hipwell, who emerged from Catchpole's shadow to assume his rightful place as a world-class player. He'd come out of retirement to make that second tour; he was backed up by world-class forwards like Mark Loane, Tony Shaw and Greg Cornelsen. Also in the team was Paul McLean, the latest, along with lock Peter McLean, of the long

line of rugby-playing McLeans, the most famous rugby family in Australia.

Even when the 1981-82 Wallabies returned home, some players went to league – a continuing problem which Australian rugby has learned to live with and tolerate, however unsatisfactory it is to the union code to see the best young players switch just when they are about to play their best rugby.

The Future

While Japan, Canada, the United States, the Fijians and Tongans all have taken up rugby with great enthusiasm, it was obvious in the early 1980s that Romania and Argentina were going to be the two countries to challenge the International Board – the home countries, France, New Zealand, South Africa and Australia. And with South Africa in near exile, the emerging countries took full advantage of their absence to fulfil cancelled schedules and tours.

All of these countries had come to Britain at some time or other, with the Argentinians making a great impact in 1976, losing to a full-strength Welsh XV only by a last-minute penalty. None of the home countries enjoyed touring there, either; the Pumas are an aggressive, if sometimes undisciplined, lot and it was a

measure of England's regard for them that they awarded full caps on their 1981 tour, which was led by Bill Beaumont.

Romania are pressing to be included in the International Championship, while Argentina want International Board status. There's a lot more to acceptance than 80 minutes' play on the field and it's generally thought that they'll have to wait a few more years to enter the inner sanctums.

Wales playing Australia in the tour of 1975-76. This was a poor tour for the Wallabies, as they lost three of the four Tests.

Andy Ripley bursts away with the ball despite a tackle. The 1974 Lions playing the Leopards in South Africa.

The Origins of the League

David Howes

Rugby became a divided game in a contest with the final score ... Amateurs 282, Semi-professionals 136.

The historic battle was played out, not on a grass pitch, but in a room in London housing the annual general meeting of the Rugby Football Union on 20 September, 1893.

The confrontation was staged against a backcloth of rising discontent in the North of England where the basically working class players were seeking 'broken time' payments for loss of earnings as a result of taking time off work to play the 15-a-side code.

In opposition were the southern-based players, predominantly recruited from university and public school backgrounds, who could more easily afford the time and money to enjoy the sport. Accusations were being freely kicked about that missed work shifts were being recompensed by the northern clubs.

At the AGM it was proposed by Mr J. A. Miller, President of the Yorkshire RFU, that players could be compensated for *bona fide* loss of time. The Secretary of the Union immediately counter-proposed that this move be halted as it was against the amateur spirit of the game.

The resultant vote brought the overwhelming victory for the establishment and further stringent measures were brought in during the next two years to curb any threat of payment to players. The split was becoming a chasm.

The inevitable occurred on 29 August, 1895, when 21 clubs from Lancashire and Yorkshire attended a special meeting in the George Hotel in Huddersfield, the heart of the industrial North. Only Dewsbury did not vote in favour of the formation of the Northern Rugby Football Union, the roots of the family tree of Rugby League.

The 20 founder member clubs featured 11 from the White Rose county – Batley, Bradford, Brighouse Rangers, Halifax, Huddersfield, Hull, Hunslet, Leeds, Liversedge, Manningham and Wakefield Trinity – with the remaining nine clubs from west of the Pennines – Broughton Rangers, Leigh, Oldham, Rochdale, St Helens, Tyldesley, Warrington, Wigan and Widnes.

Cheshire clubs Runcorn and Stockport joined the pioneers for the inaugural season. A maximum payment of 6/- (30p) a day was permitted as broken time recompense with all players having to be employed outside of the game. The campaigning administrators insisted that the northern game operate on a part-time basis, a code of conduct which is still applied today.

A fundamental change in principle took place during this transitional period, the northern code consciously becoming a spectator sport rather than one designed purely for participation.

After two years of playing to the traditional Rugby Union rules, the northern bosses sought crowd appeal and scrapped the line-out, altered the scoring system to three points for a try and two for a goal and, in doing so, dug the foundations for the development of the game of Rugby League.

As with any spectator sport, the competitive element became of paramount importance. The parochial Yorkshire and Lancashire Competitions were scrapped in favour of a new set-up powered through by the 12 most influential clubs. The formation of the competition gave birth to a new title ... The Northern Rugby League.

This important breakthrough came in 1901, four years after the birth of the Challenge Cup competition which all the clubs entered. It was organised on a knockout basis, Batley beating St Helens at Leeds in the first Final on 1 May 1897, 13,490 people paying £624 to watch.

The most fundamental change to the

rules came in 1906 when it was decided to try to inspire more open, flowing play. The two wing forwards were made redundant and while Rugby Union continued with its 15-a-side format, Rugby League became 13-a-side.

In just 10 years the broken time issue had initiated a new code of rugby with an individual style of competition and play, a part-time professional sport being well supported by the paying public.

Like a rolling snowball, the new version of rugby began to gain momentum . . . at home and abroad. The legendary A. H. Baskerville and George Smith brought the touring 'All Blacks' over from New Zealand in 1907, winning 19 of the 35 tour matches. A year later an Australian side followed their footsteps, winning 19 and drawing six of their 46 tour matches. In 1910 the first Great Britain tour party sailed round the world for a highly successful return visit.

Inside only three years the northern-based game of Rugby League had found worldwide fame and fortune. But while the game continued to grow down under, progress stuttered on home shores.

Wales became a growth area, with Ebbw Vale and Merthyr Tydfil joining the part-time sport in 1907, to be followed a year later by Aberdare, Treherbert, Mid Rhondda and Barry. The Union stronghold held firm and by 1914 the new code had been and gone.

The final act of separation came at the AGM of 1922 when the northern game established its own identity with the adoption of the title The Rugby Football League. In 1928 the Rugby League Council rubbed salt into the wound by taking the bold decision to stage the showpiece Challenge Cup Final at Wembley, the heart of Rugby Union country. Amid controversy at both ends of the country, the 1929 Final between Dewsbury and Wigan set the pattern for an annual pilgrimage to the Empire Stadium.

As with Britain, New Zealand and Australia, disharmony in the Rugby Union ranks paved the way for the formation of the French Rugby League. The famous Jean Galia brought over a band of tourists in 1933 and the following August Rugby a Treize was officially born in France.

From this boom start, Rugby League in Britain prospered in the post-Second World War era. The 1950s and 1960s trend

towards participation sports forced some radical rule changes, the improvement of social facilities and a switch from Saturday to Sunday fixtures.

Rugby League became a television sport, the first national broadcast being the Great Britain v New Zealand Second Test at Swinton on 10 November 1951. Inevitably sponsorship followed, and in the 1980s the League is attracting £300,000 per year from the world of commerce.

A change of hierarchy and attitude in the mid-1970s brought about a mini-boom culminating in the birth of three new clubs, all sharing grounds with soccer outfits, Fulham being the pioneers in 1980-81, followed a year later by Carlisle and Cardiff City.

Halifax Rugby League team of 1950. The players are, back: E. MacDonald, F. R. Birkin, L. Olsen. Centre: D. Hatfield, A. Ackerley, G. Price, D. Stokes, H. Greenwood. Front: L. Falcon, D. Chalkley, L. White, S. Kielty, K. Dean.

Billy Boston, one of the great three-quarters of Rugby League, making a run in the World Cup Final at Odsal Stadium, Bradford, in 1960. Great Britain beat Australia 10-3.

The Rugby League Challenge Cup winners of 1980, Hull Kingston Rovers. The final at Wembley each year is a big Rugby League occasion.

Below *Two of the newest Rugby League clubs in opposition.* Fulham (black with white V) *began in 1980 and Carlisle a year later.*

The Rugby League Clubs

David Howes

A roll call of the great clubs in Rugby League history would find lowly BATLEY one of the last to come to mind.

Yet the West Yorkshire club, whose Mount Pleasant ground is perched high on a windswept hill, took the game by storm in its formative years. Batley claimed a place in the annals by becoming the first winners of the coveted Challenge Cup, then known as the Northern Union Cup, back in 1897. Having beaten St Helens 10-3 at Headingley, Leeds, they returned a year later to dispose of Bradford and made it three victories out of the first five finals by beating Warrington at the same venue in 1901.

They enjoyed a second purple patch between 1922 and 1925, including the 1923-24 Championship title, to earn the respected nickname 'The Gallant Youths'. Apart from being runners-up in the 1952-53 Yorkshire Cup Final, Batley have never scaled the heights again and in recent years have battled in the basement of the 13-a-side code.

Neighbours BRADFORD NORTHERN have, by contrast, amassed 28 title successes in a chequered existence clouded by reformations of the club. The original Bradford played at Park Avenue as one of the founder members of the Northern Union until 1907, when financial losses brought an unsuccessful attempt to return to Rugby Union, before switching to soccer.

During this initial spell the club had tasted success with Challenge Cup and Championship titles. On 24 May 1907, a new club, entitled Bradford Northern, was formed from the dying embers of the Park Avenue set-up. After a year at Greenfield, the new club moved to Birch Lane, a poverty stricken venue which was to be home for the next 26 years. That quarter of a century was spent struggling for existence before the club moved to its present home of Odsal Stadium.

The local corporation had created a large bowl at Odsal Top by tipping rubbish and the first Rugby League game was staged on 1 September 1934 with Huddersfield as the visitors.

The move heralded the start of Northern's most successful era with Odsal housing a world record 102,569 for the Challenge Cup replay between Warrington and Halifax in 1954; the emergence of legendary figures such as Ernest Ward, Frank Whitcombe, Eric Batten, Ken Traill, W. H. T. Davies and Trevor Foster; and a record three appearances at Wembley between 1947-49.

Lean years returned in the mid-1950s and in 1963-64 the club folded only to be re-formed yet again at the start of the 1964-65 season. Northern became known as one of the most flamboyant clubs in the League and once again became a force in the game reaching Wembley in 1973 and lifting the Championship title in successive seasons in 1980 and 1981, adding to the Second Division title of 1974.

HUDDERSFIELD were one of the founder members of the breakaway movement of 1895, the historic meeting being held in the town. Yet, ironically, the local team did not figure in the title of the club which is the Huddersfield Cricket and Athletic Club!

Until the mid-1960s, the Fartown club were one of the forces in the game lifting a total of 37 titles, including the Championship seven times and the Challenge Cup six times. Included on the club payroll were such famous figures as the legendary Harold Wagstaff who made his début as a 15-year-old in 1906; Australians Lionel Cooper, Pat Devery and Johnny Hunter; Scotsmen Dave Valentine, Jock Anderson and David Rose; Irishman Jack Daly; Kiwi sprinter Peter Henderson; Welshmen Billy Banks, Ike Owens and Bill Griffin; plus local talent Ron Rylance, Jim Bowden and Russ Pepperell.

To that list one can add club record holders Ben Gronow, with 147 goals and 330 points in 1919-20, and the world famous Albert Rosenfield who touched down 80 times in 1913-14 for a world record tally of tries.

Elsewhere in Yorkshire, HULL are the current boom club, attracting the biggest gates and, along with neighbours and arch-rivals Hull Kingston Rovers, spending the most money in the transfer market. One of the oldest clubs, Hull purchased their Boulevard home in 1899 and the pitch has played host to many great names including Billy Batten, Joe Oliver, Bob Taylor, Tommy Harris, Johnny Whiteley, the Drake twins, Clive Sullivan and, in the present era, Steve Norton.

Over the River Hull at Craven Park, HULL KINGSTON ROVERS, after an almost solitary spell of success in the early 1920s, have emerged as one of today's top sides, the emergence from the doldrums coinciding with the capture of Roger Millward in 1966, the mini-maestro now having graduated to coach. They have lifted four major trophies in the past four years and broken the world record transfer fee three times for Phil Hogan (£35,000), Len Casey (£38,000) and George Fairbairn (£72,500).

LEEDS shares a sporting complex which stages both Rugby League and cricket at Test level. The Loiners have always been one of the game's quality sides, reflected by their 53 title successes spread consistently over their long history as founder members of the game. Their quest for the highest standards is reflected in their ground, with the game's only undersoil heating system, and their players' roll call, which includes the likes of Arthur Clues, Lewis Jones, Eric Harris, Vic Hey, Jim Brough, Stan Brogden, Fred Harris, Bert Cook, Dicky Williams, Jeff Stevenson, and more recently, Ray Batten, Bev Risman, John Atkinson, Syd Hynes, John Holmes and current International captain David Ward.

Linked with a church society which gives rise to the club name, WAKEFIELD TRINITY have also put the White Rose county on the sporting map. The meeting of Leeds and Trinity at Wembley in the 1968 Cup Final will always be remembered, both for the watersplash conditions and the last-second missed goal by Don Fox which would have sent the cup back to Wakefield.

Trinity moved to their Belle Vue home in 1879 and in the early part of this century their star name was the great Jonty Parkin, one of the legends of the game. In the 1960s, Trinity's most successful period, they reached Wembley four times, losing only once . . . that memorable 1968 Final. From the earlier eras the names of Parkin, Mick Exley, Charlie Pollard and Herbert Goodfellow will be remembered. But it was the latter period which produced a string of great names highlighted by Neil Fox, Jack Wilkinson, Derek Turner, Harold Poynton, Fred Smith, Gerry Round, Alan Skene and Ken Traill.

Over in Lancashire, Rugby League has made the glass-producing town of ST HELENS a household name. Pioneers of the breakaway movement, the Saints came to the fore between 1925 and 1935 with stars in Alf Ellaby, Leslie Fairclough, Alf Frodsham and Ben Halfpenny. After the Second World War, they recruited Glyn Moses, Doug Silcock and Alan Prescott.

In 1958, the Great Britain touring side contained six Saints .. Moses, Prescott, Frank Carlton, Alex Murphy, Vince Karalius and Abe Terry. Also in the line-up through the 1960s and 1970s were the likes of Dick Huddart, Tommy Bishop, Tom Van Vollenhoven, Kel Coslett, John Mantle, Jan Prinsloo, Cliff Watson and Ray French, now BBC TV Rugby League commentator.

Finally, the club which is synonomous with Rugby League . . . WIGAN. The holders of most titles – 54 – the Central Park club have been the stalwarts of the game with only short periods barren of success. Their illustrious history has been peppered with great names in great teams . . . Jim Leytham, Jim Sullivan, Lance Todd, Cec Mountford, Johnny Ring, Billy Boston, Tommy Bradshaw, Eric Ashton and Martin Ryan.

The strength of Wigan was typified in 1950 when eight star players set off for a tour of Australia and the reserves helped the club to finish top of the table and win the Championship Final!

The modern-day Red Rose spotlight has fallen on the less fashionable WIDNES, who since 1971 have figured in 23 finals, winning 12. The Widnes record of six appearances in the last eight Challenge Cup finals inspired this graffito accolade on a wall on the border of the town: 'Widnes . . . . . twin town Wembley'.

BARROW

Ground: Craven Park
Colours: Royal blue jerseys, blue shorts
First Season: 1900-01
Nickname: Shipbuilders
Honours: **Challenge Cup** Winners, 1954-55
Beaten finalists, 1937-38, 1950-51,
1956-57, 1966-67
John Player Trophy Beaten finalists
1980-81
Lancashire Cup Winners, 1954-55
Beaten finalists, 1937-38
Division Two Champions, 1975-76
Records: Attendance: 21,651 v. Salford
(League) 15 April, 1938
Goals: 135 by J. Ball, 1956-57
Tries: 50 by J. Lewthwaite, 1956-57
Points: 305 by Ian Ball, 1979-80

BATLEY

Ground: Mount Pleasant
Colours: Cerise and fawn jerseys, cerise shorts
First Season: 1895-96
Nickname: Gallant Youths
Honours: **Championship** Winners, 1923-24
Challenge Cup Winners, 1896-97,
1897-98, 1900-01
Yorkshire League Winners, 1898-99,
1923-24
Yorkshire Cup Winners, 1912-13
Beaten finalists, 1909-10, 1922-23,
1924-25, 1952-53
Records: Attendance: 23,989 v. Leeds
(RL Cup) 14 March, 1925
Goals: 120 by S. Thompson, 1958-59
Tries: 29 by J. Tindall, 1912-13
Points: 281 by J. Perry, 1950-51

BLACKPOOL BOROUGH

Ground: Borough Park
Colours: Black jerseys with green shoulder
panel, black shorts
First Season: 1954-55
Nickname: Milers
Honours: **John Player Trophy** Beaten finalists,
1976-77
Records: Attendance: 7,614 v. Castleford
(RL Cup) March 14, 1964. There was
an attendance of 21,000 in an RL
Cup-tie against Leigh on Blackpool
AFC ground in 1957.
Goals: 89 by J. Maughan, 1958-59
Tries: 22 by J. Johnson, 1970-71
Points: 201 by P. Fearis, 1957-58

BRADFORD NORTHERN

Ground: Odsal Stadium
Colours: White jerseys with red, amber and
black hoops, white shorts
First Season: 1895-96 as 'Bradford'. Disbanded and
became Bradford Northern in 1907-08.
Disbanded during 1963-64 and re-
formed for start of 1964-65

Nickname: Northern
Honours: **Challenge Cup** Winners, 1905-06,
1943-44, 1946-47, 1948-49
Beaten finalists, 1897-98, 1944-45,
1947-48, 1972-73
Championship Beaten finalists,
1947-48, 1951-52
Division One Champions, 1903-04,
1979-80, 1980-81
Division Two Champions, 1973-74
War-time Emergency League
Championship winners, 1939-40,
1940-41
Yorkshire League Winners,
1899-1900, 1900-01, 1939-40, 1940-41,
1940-41, 1944-45. Beaten finalists,
1941-42.
Yorkshire Cup Winners, 1906-07,
1940-41, 1941-42, 1943-44, 1945-46,
1948-49, 1949-50, 1953-54, 1965-66,
1978-79
Beaten finalists, 1913-14
Premiership Winners, 1977-78
Beaten finalists, 1978-79, 1979-80
John Player Trophy Winners,
1974-75, 1979-80
Records: Attendance: 102,569 Warrington v.
Halifax (RL Cup Final replay) 5 May,
1954
Goals: 173 by E. Tees, 1971-72
Tries: 63 by J. McLean, 1951-52
Points: 364 by E. Tees, 1971-72

BRAMLEY

Ground: McLaren Field
Colours: Amber jerseys with black collar, cuffs
and V, black shorts
First Season: 1896-97
Nickname: Villagers
Honours: **BBC2 Floodlit Trophy** Winners,
1973-74
Records: Attendance: 12,600 v. Leeds (League)
7 May, 1947
Goals: 130 by J. Wilson, 1961-62
Tries: 20 by A. Smith, 1972-73
Points: 260 by J. Wilson, 1961-62

CARDIFF CITY

Ground: Ninian Park
Colours: Blue jerseys with yellow V, blue shorts
First Season: 1981-82. A Cardiff team competed in
the 1951-52 campaign
Nickname: Blue Dragons
Records: Attendance: 9,247 v. Salford (Div 2),
30 August, 1981
Goals: 109 by S. Fenwick, 1981-82
Tries: 14 by R. Fleay, 1981-82
Points: 256 by S. Fenwick, 1981-82

CARLISLE

Ground: Brunton Park
Colours: Blue jerseys with red and white band,
white shorts
First Season: 1981-82. A Carlisle City team entered
the League in 1928-29 but withdrew
after 10 matches, winning one

Records: Attendance: 5,903 v. Workington Town (Div 2), 6 September, 1981
Goals: 113 by S. Ferres, 1981-82
Tries: 25 by M. Morgan, 1981-82
Points: 242 by S. Ferres, 1981-82

CASTLEFORD

Ground: Wheldon Road

Colours: Yellow jerseys with black collar and cuffs, black shorts

First Season: 1926-27. There was also a Castleford team from 1896-97 to 1905-06, inclusive

Nickname: Glassblowers

Honours: **Championship** Beaten finalists, 1938-39, 1968-69
Challenge Cup Winners, 1934-35, 1968-69, 1969-70
Yorkshire League Winners, 1932-33, 1938-39, 1964-65
Yorkshire Cup Winners, 1977-78
Beaten finalists, 1948-49, 1950-51, 1968-69, 1971-72, 1981-82
Eastern Division Championship Beaten finalists, 1963-64
BBC2 Floodlit Trophy Winners, 1965-66, 1966-67, 1967-68, 1976-77
John Player Trophy Winners, 1976-77

Records: Attendance: 25,449 v. Hunslet (RL Cup) 3 March, 1935
Goals: 158 by S. Lloyd, 1976-77
Tries: 36 by K. Howe, 1963-64
Points: 331 by S. Lloyd, 1976-77

Opposite top *John Joyner of Castleford, with the Yorkshire Cup, won after beating Bradford Northern in 1982.*

Opposite bottom *Two stalwart Lancashire sides clashing in 1979, Warrington and Wigan. Wigan's Les Bolton making a pass.*

Left *The two Hull sides, Hull* (irregular black and white hoops) *and Hull Kingston Rovers* (white with red band) *playing each other in the Rugby League Challenge Cup Final, 1980.*

Below *Bradford Northern* (in red) *and Widnes in May 1979 with their trophies. The two clubs won seven trophies in all.*

DEWSBURY

Ground: Crown Flatt
Colours: Red, amber and black jerseys, white shorts
First Season: 1901-02
Honours: **Championship** Winners, 1972-73
Beaten finalists, 1946-47
Division Two Champions, 1904-05
Challenge Cup Winners, 1911-12, 1942-43
Beaten finalists, 1928-29
Yorkshire League Winners, 1946-47
Yorkshire Cup Winners, 1925-26, 1927-28, 1942-43
Beaten finalists, 1918-19, 1921-22, 1940-41, 1972-73
BBC2 Floodlit Trophy Beaten finalists, 1975-76
War League Championship Winners, 1941-42
Records: Attendance: 26,584 v. Halifax (Yorkshire Cup) 30 October, 1920
Goals: 145 by N. Stephenson, 1972-73
Tries: 40 by D. Thomas, 1906-07
Points: 368 by N. Stephenson, 1972-73

DONCASTER

Ground: Tattersfield
Colours: White jerseys with blue and gold bands, white shorts
First Season: 1951-52
Nickname: Dons
Records: Attendance: 4,793 v. Wakefield T. (League) 7 April, 1962
Goals: 91 by D. Noble, 1981-82
Tries: 18 by John Buckton, 1981-82
Points: 187 by T. Griffiths, 1951-52

FEATHERSTONE ROVERS

Ground: Post Office Road
Colours: Blue and white hooped jerseys, blue shorts
First Season: 1921-22
Nickname: Colliers
Honours: **Challenge Cup** Winners, 1966-67, 1972-73
Runners-up, 1951-52, 1973-74
Championship Beaten finalists, 1927-28
Division One Champions, 1976-77
Division Two Champions, 1979-80
Yorkshire Cup Winners, 1939-40, 1959-60
Beaten finalists, 1928-29, 1963-64, 1966-67, 1969-70, 1970-71, 1976-77, 1977-78
Captain Morgan Trophy Beaten finalists, 1973-74
Records: Attendance: 17,531 v. St Helens (RL Cup) 21 March, 1959
Goals: 163 by S. Quinn, 1979-80
Tries: 31 by C. Woolford, 1958-59
Points: 375 by S. Quinn, 1979-80

FULHAM

Ground: Craven Cottage
Colours: Black jerseys with red and white chevron, black shorts
First Season: 1980-81
Records: Attendance: 15,013 v. Wakefield T. (RL Cup) 15 February, 1981
Goals: 93 by S. Diamond, 1981-82
Tries: 16 by M. Aspey, 1980-81
Points: 206 by S. Diamond, 1981-82

HALIFAX

Ground: Thrum Hall
Colours: Blue and white hooped jerseys, white shorts
First Season: 1895-96
Nickname: Thrum Hallers
Honours: **Championship** Winners, 1906-07, 1964-65
Beaten finalists, 1952-53, 1953-54, 1955-56, 1965-66
Division One Champions, 1902-03
Challenge Cup Winners, 1902-03, 1903-04, 1930-31, 1938-39
Beaten finalists, 1920-21, 1940-41, 1941-42, 1948-49, 1953-54, 1955-56
Yorkshire League Winners, 1908-09, 1920-21, 1952-53, 1953-54, 1955-56, 1957-58
Eastern Division Championship Winners, 1963-64
Yorkshire Cup Winners, 1908-09, 1944-45, 1954-55, 1955-56, 1963-64
Beaten finalists, 1905-06, 1907-08, 1941-42, 1979-80
John Player Trophy Winners, 1971-72
Records: Attendance: 29,153 v. Wigan (RL Cup) 21 March, 1959
Goals: 147 by T. Griffiths, 1955-56
Tries: 48 by J. Freeman, 1956-57
Points: 297 by T. Griffiths, 1955-56

HUDDERSFIELD

Ground: Fartown
Colours: Claret and gold hooped jerseys, white shorts
First Season: 1895-96
Honours: **Championship** Winners, 1911-12, 1912-13, 1914-15, 1928-29, 1929-30, 1948-49, 1961-62
Beaten finalists, 1913-14, 1919-20, 1922-23, 1931-32, 1945-46, 1949-50
Division Two Champions, 1974-75
Challenge Cup Winners, 1912-13, 1914-15, 1919-20, 1932-33, 1944-45, 1952-53
Beaten finalists, 1934-35, 1961-62
Yorkshire League Winners, 1911-12, 1912-13, 1913-14, 1914-15, 1919-20, 1921-22, 1928-29, 1929-30, 1948-49, 1949-50, 1951-52
Eastern Division Beaten finalists, 1962-63

Yorkshire Cup Winners, 1909-10, 1911-12, 1913-14, 1914-15, 1918-19, 1919-20, 1926-27, 1931-32, 1938-39, 1950-51, 1952-53, 1957-58
Beaten finalists, 1910-11, 1923-24, 1925-26, 1930-31, 1937-38, 1942-43, 1949-50, 1960-61

Records: Attendance: 35,136 Leeds v. Wakefield T. (RL Cup SF) 19 April, 1947
Goals: 147 by B. Gronow, 1919-20
Tries: 80 by A. Rosenfeld, 1913-14
Points: 330 by B. Gronow, 1919-20

Left Steve Norton, playing against Leigh in the 1980-81 season. Norton is one of Hull's strongest and most inventive players.

HULL

Ground: The Boulevard
Colours: Irregular black and white hooped jerseys, white shorts
First Season: 1895-96
Nickname: Airlie Birds
Honours: **Championship** Winners, 1919-20, 1920-21, 1935-36, 1955-56, 1957-58
Beaten finalists, 1956-57
Division Two Champions, 1976-77, 1978-79
Challenge Cup Winners, 1913-14, 1981-82
Beaten finalists, 1907-08, 1908-09, 1909-10, 1921-22, 1922-23, 1958-59, 1959-60, 1979-80
Yorkshire League Winners, 1918-19, 1922-23, 1926-27, 1935-36
Yorkshire Cup Winners, 1923-24, 1969-70
Beaten finalists, 1912-13, 1914-15, 1920-21, 1927-28, 1938-39, 1946-47, 1953-54, 1954-55, 1955-56, 1959-60, 1967-68
John Player Trophy Winners, 1981-82
Beaten finalists, 1975-76
BBC2 Floodlit Trophy Winners, 1979-80
Premiership Beaten finalists, 1980-81

Records: Attendance: 28,798 v. Leeds (RL Cup) 7 March 1936
Goals: 170 by S. Lloyd, 1978-79
Tries: 52 by J. Harrison, 1914-15
Points: 369 by S. Lloyd, 1978-79

Below Hull Kingston Rovers' Fairbairn making a run against Swinton. At £72,500 he is the League record signing.

HULL KINGSTON ROVERS

Ground: Craven Park
Colours: White jerseys with red band, white shorts
First Season: 1899-1900
Nickname: Robins
Honours: **Championship** Winners, 1922-23, 1924-25
Beaten finalists, 1920-21, 1967-68
First Division Champions, 1978-79
Challenge Cup Winners, 1979-80
Beaten finalists, 1904-05, 1924-25, 1963-64, 1980-81
Premiership Winners, 1980-81
John Player Trophy Beaten finalists, 1981-82
Yorkshire League Winners, 1924-25, 1925-26

David Heron in the blue and amber of Leeds playing against Widnes in 1982.

Championship Winners, 1907-08, 1937-38
Beaten finalists, 1958-59
Division Two Champions, 1962-63
Yorkshire Cup Winners, 1905-06, 1907-08, 1962-63
Beaten finalists, 1908-09, 1929-30, 1931-32, 1944-45, 1956-57, 1965-66
Yorkshire League Winners, 1897-98, 1907-08, 1931-32

Records: Attendance: 24,700 v. Wigan (RL Cup), 15 March, 1924
Goals: 181 by W. Langton, 1958-59
Tries: 34 by A. Snowden, 1956-57
Points: 380 by W. Langton, 1958-59

HUYTON

Ground: Alt Park
Colours: Black jerseys with red collar, black shorts
First Season: 1922-23 as Wigan Highfield. Became London Highfield in 1933-34. Became Liverpool Stanley in 1934-35 and changed to Liverpool City in 1951-52. Huyton began at the start of 1968-69.
There was also a Liverpool City in 1906-07.
Honours: **Lancashire League** Winners, 1935-36
Records: Attendance: 14,000 v. Widnes (Championship semi-final) 2 May, 1936
Goals: 97 by S. Oakley, 1933-34
Tries: 28 by J. Maloney, 1930-31
Points: 211 by J. Wood, 1954-55

KEIGHLEY

Ground: Lawkholme Lane
Colours: White jerseys with scarlet and emerald green V, white shorts
First Season: 1901-02
Nickname: Lawkholmers
Honours: **Division Two** Champions, 1902-03
Challenge Cup Beaten finalists, 1936-37
Yorkshire Cup Beaten finalists, 1943-44, 1951-52
Records: Attendance: 14,500 v. Halifax (RL Cup) 3 March, 1951
Goals: 155 by B. Jefferson, 1973-74
Tries: 30 by J. Sherburn, 1934-35
Points: 331 by B. Jefferson, 1973-74

Yorkshire Cup Winners, 1920-21, 1929-30, 1966-67, 1967-68, 1971-72, 1974-75
Beaten finalists, 1906-07, 1911-12, 1933-34, 1962-63, 1975-76, 1980-81
BBC2 Floodlit Trophy Winners, 1977-78
Beaten finalists, 1979-80
Eastern Division Championship Winners, 1962-63
Records: Attendance: 22,282 v. Hull, 7 October, 1922
Goals: 166 by G. Fairbairn, 1981-82
Tries: 42 by G. Dunn, 1974-75
Points: 366 by S. Hubbard, 1979-80

HUNSLET

Ground: Leeds United AFC, Elland Road
Colours: Myrtle, flame and white jerseys, white shorts
First Season: 1895-96. Disbanded at end of 1972-73. Re-formed as New Hunslet in 1973-74. Retitled Hunslet from start of 1979-80
Honours: **Challenge Cup** Winners, 1907-08, 1933-34
Beaten finalists, 1898-99, 1964-65

LEEDS

Ground: Headingley
Colours: Blue and amber jerseys, white shorts
First Season: 1895-96
Nickname: Loiners
Honours: **Championship** Winners, 1960-61, 1968-69, 1971-72
Beaten finalists, 1914-15, 1928-29, 1929-30, 1930-31, 1937-38, 1969-70, 1972-73
League Leaders Trophy Winners, 1966-67, 1967-68, 1968-69, 1969-70, 1971-72

Challenge Cup Winners, 1909-10, 1922-23, 1931-32, 1935-36, 1940-41, 1941-42, 1956-57, 1967-68, 1976-77, 1977-78
Beaten finalists, 1942-43, 1946-47, 1970-71, 1971-72
Yorkshire League Winners, 1901-02, 1927-28, 1930-31, 1933-34, 1934-35, 1936-37, 1937-38, 1950-51, 1954-55, 1956-57, 1960-61, 1966-67, 1967-68, 1968-69, 1969-70
Yorkshire Cup Winners, 1921-22, 1928-29, 1930-31, 1932-33, 1934-35, 1935-36, 1937-38, 1958-59, 1968-69, 1970-71, 1972-73, 1973-74, 1975-76, 1976-77, 1979-80, 1980-81
Beaten finalists, 1919-20, 1947-48, 1961-62, 1964-65
BBC2 Floodlit Trophy Winners, 1970-71
John Player Trophy Winners, 1972-73
Premiership Winners, 1974-75, 1978-79

Records: Attendance: 40,175 v. Bradford N. (League) 21 March, 1947
Goals: 166 by L. Jones, 1956-57
Tries: 63 by E. Harris, 1935-36
Points: 431 by L. Jones, 1956-57

LEIGH

Ground: Hilton Park
Colours: Cherry and white jerseys, white shorts
First Season: 1895-96
Honours: **Championship** Winners, 1905-06
Division One Champions, 1981-82
Division Two Champions, 1977-78
Challenge Cup Winners, 1920-21, 1970-71
Lancashire Cup Winners, 1952-53, 1955-56, 1970-71
Beaten finalists, 1905-06, 1909-10, 1920-21, 1922-23, 1949-50, 1951-52, 1963-64, 1969-70
BBC2 Trophy Winners, 1969-70, 1972-73
Beaten finalists, 1967-68, 1976-77

Records: Attendance: 31,324 v. St Helens (RL Cup) 14 March, 1953
Goals: 166 by S. Ferguson, 1970-71
Tries: 36 by W. Kindon, 1956-57
Points: 356 by S. Ferguson, 1970-71

OLDHAM

Ground: Watersheddings
Colours: Red and white hooped jerseys, red sleeves, white shorts
First Season: 1895-96
Nickname: Roughyeds
Honours: **Championship** Winners, 1909-10, 1910-11, 1956-57
Beaten finalists, 1906-07, 1907-08, 1908-09, 1921-22, 1954-55
Division One Champions, 1904-05
Division Two Champions, 1963-64, 1981-82

Leigh playing Hull in 1980-81. The cherry and white shirt is worn by Eddie Bowman.

Challenge Cup Winners, 1898-99, 1924-25, 1926-27
Beaten finalists, 1906-07, 1911-12, 1923-24, 1925-26
Lancashire League Winners, 1897-98, 1900-01, 1907-08, 1909-10, 1921-22, 1956-57, 1957-58
Lancashire Cup Winners, 1907-08, 1910-11, 1913-14, 1919-20, 1924-25, 1933-34, 1956-57, 1957-58, 1958-59
Beaten finalists, 1908-09, 1911-12, 1918-19, 1921-22, 1954-55, 1966-67, 1968-69

Records: Attendance: 28,000 v. Huddersfield (League) 24 February, 1912
Goals: 200 by B. Ganley, 1957-58
Tries: 49 by R. Farrar, 1921-22
Points: 412 by B. Ganley, 1957-58

ROCHDALE HORNETS

Ground: Athletic Grounds
Colours: White jerseys with blue and red band, white shorts
First Season: 1895-96
Nickname: Hornets
Honours: **Challenge Cup** Winners, 1921-22

Lancashire League Winners,
1918-19
Lancashire Cup Winners, 1911-12,
1914-15, 1918-19
Beaten finalists, 1912-13, 1919-20,
1965-66
John Player Trophy Beaten finalists,
1973-74
BBC2 Floodlit Trophy Beaten
finalists, 1971-72

Records: Attendance: 41,831 Wigan v. Oldham
(RL Cup Final) 12 April, 1924
Goals: 107 by W. Holliday, 1973-74
Tries: 30 by J. Williams, 1934-35
Points: 235 by G. Starkey, 1966-67

ST HELENS

Ground: Knowsley Road
Colours: White jerseys with red V, white shorts
First Season: 1895-96
Nickname: Saints
Honours: **Championship** Winners, 1931-32,
1952-53, 1958-59, 1965-66, 1969-70,
1970-71
Beaten finalists, 1964-65, 1966-67,
1971-72
Division One Champions, 1974-75
League Leaders Trophy Winners,
1964-65, 1965-66
Club Championship (Merit Table)
Beaten finalists, 1973-74
Challenge Cup Winners, 1955-56,
1960-61, 1965-66, 1971-72, 1975-76
Beaten finalists, 1896-97, 1914-15,
1929-30, 1952-53, 1977-78
Lancashire Cup Winners, 1926-27,
1953-54, 1960-61, 1961-62, 1962-63,
1963-64, 1964-65, 1967-68, 1968-69
Beaten finalists, 1932-33, 1952-53,
1956-57, 1958-59, 1959-60, 1970-71
Lancashire League Winners,
1929-30, 1931-32, 1952-53, 1959-60,
1964-65, 1965-66, 1966-67, 1968-69
Premiership Winners, 1975-76,
1976-77
Beaten finalists, 1974-75
Western Division Championship
Winners, 1963-64
BBC2 Trophy Winners, 1971-72,
1975-76
Beaten finalists, 1965-66, 1968-69,
1970-71, 1977-78, 1978-79

Records: Attendance: 35,695 v. Wigan
(League) 26 December, 1949
Goals: 214 by K. Coslett, 1971-72
Tries: 62 by T. Van Vollenhoven,
1958-59
Points: 452 by K. Coslett, 1971-72

SALFORD

Ground: The Willows
Colours: Red jerseys, white shorts
First Season: 1896-97
Nickname: Red Devils
Honours: **Championship** Winners, 1913-14,
1932-33, 1936-37, 1938-39
Beaten finalists, 1933-34

Division One Champions, 1973-74,
1975-76
Challenge Cup Winners, 1937-38
Beaten finalists, 1899-1900, 1901-02,
1902-03, 1905-06, 1938-39, 1968-69
Lancashire League Winners,
1932-33, 1933-34, 1934-35, 1936-37,
1938-39
Lancashire Cup Winners, 1931-32,
1934-35, 1935-36, 1936-37, 1972-73
Beaten finalists, 1929-30, 1938-39,
1973-74, 1974-75, 1975-76
Premiership Beaten finalists, 1975-76
John Player Trophy Beaten finalists,
1972-73
BBC2 Trophy Winners, 1974-75

Records: Attendance: 26,470 v. Warrington
(RL Cup) 13 February, 1937
Goals: 221 by D. Watkins, 1972-73
Tries: 46 by K. Fielding, 1973-74
Points: 493 by D. Watkins, 1972-73

SWINTON

Ground: Station Road
Colours: Blue jerseys with white V, white shorts
First Season: 1896-97
Nickname: Lions
Honours: **Championship** Winners 1926-27,
1927-28, 1930-31, 1934-35
Beaten finalists, 1924-25, 1932-33
War League Beaten finalists, 1939-40
Division One Champions, 1962-63,
1963-64
Challenge Cup Winners, 1899-1900,
1925-26, 1927-28
Beaten finalists, 1926-27, 1931-32
Lancashire League Winners,
1924-25, 1927-28, 1928-29, 1930-31,
1960-61
Lancashire War League Winners,
1939-40
Lancashire Cup Winners, 1925-26,
1927-28, 1939-40, 1969-70
Beaten finalists, 1910-11, 1923-24,
1931-32, 1960-61, 1961-62, 1962-63,
1964-65, 1972-73
BBC2 Trophy Beaten finalists,
1966-67
Western Division Championship
Beaten finalists, 1963-64

Records: Attendance: 44,621 Wigan v. Leigh
(Lancashire Cup Final) 27 October,
1951
Goals: 128 by A. Blan, 1960-61
Tries: 42 by J. Stopford, 1963-64
Points: 283 by A. Blan, 1960-61

WAKEFIELD TRINITY

Ground: Belle Vue
Colours: White jerseys with red and blue hoops,
white shorts
First Season: 1895-96
Nickname: Dreadnoughts
Honours: **Championship** Winners, 1966-67,
1967-68
Beaten finalists, 1959-60, 1961-62
Division Two Champions, 1903-04
Challenge Cup Winners, 1908-09,
1945-46, 1959-60, 1961-62, 1962-63

Glyn Shaw (Widnes) scores a fine try despite Colin Dixon's tackle against Salford in 1980. Keith Fielding is the Salford player arriving just too late.

Below *Determination on the face of Tony Waller, wearing the primrose and blue chevron of Warrington as he battles through against Wigan.*

Beaten finalists, 1913-14, 1967-68, 1978-79
Yorkshire League Winners, 1909-10, 1910-11, 1945-46, 1958-59, 1959-60, 1961-62, 1965-66
Yorkshire Cup Winners, 1910-11, 1924-25, 1946-47, 1947-48, 1951-52, 1956-57, 1960-61, 1961-62, 1964-65
Beaten finalists, 1926-27, 1932-33, 1934-35, 1936-37, 1939-40, 1945-46, 1958-59, 1973-74, 1974-75
John Player Trophy Beaten finalists, 1971-72

Records: Attendance: 37,906 Leeds v. Huddersfield (RL Cup SF) 21 March, 1936
Goals: 163 by N. Fox, 1961-62
Tries: 38 by F. Smith, 1959-60, D. Smith, 1973-74
Points: 407 by N. Fox, 1961-62

WARRINGTON

Ground: Wilderspool
Colours: White jerseys with primrose and blue chevron, white shorts
First Season: 1895-96
Nickname: Wire
Honours: **Championship** Winners, 1947-48, 1953-54, 1954-55
Beaten finalists, 1925-26, 1934-35, 1936-37, 1948-49, 1950-51, 1960-61
League Leaders Trophy Winners, 1972-73
Club Championship (Merit Table) Winners, 1973-74
Premiership Beaten finalists, 1976-77
Challenge Cup Winners, 1904-05, 1906-07, 1949-50, 1953-54, 1973-74
Beaten finalists, 1900-01, 1903-04, 1912-13, 1927-28, 1932-33, 1935-36, 1974-75

Widnes, in the white shirts, playing Salford, in the hoops, in a Centenary match. Salford's Frank Wilson is well and truly tackled.

Lancashire League Winners, 1937-38, 1947-48, 1948-49, 1950-51, 1953-54, 1954-55, 1955-56, 1967-68
Lancashire Cup Winners, 1921-22, 1929-30, 1932-33, 1937-38, 1959-60, 1965-66, 1980-81
Beaten finalists, 1906-07, 1948-49, 1950-51, 1967-68
John Player Trophy Winners, 1973-74, 1977-78, 1980-81
Beaten finalists, 1978-79
Captain Morgan Trophy Winners, 1973-74
BBC2 Trophy Beaten finalists, 1974-75

Records: Attendance: 34,304 v. Wigan (League) 22 January, 1949
Goals: 170 by S. Hesford, 1978-79
Tries: 66 by B. Bevan, 1952-53
Points: 363 by H. Bath, 1952-53

WHITEHAVEN

Ground: Recreation Ground
Colours: White jerseys with chocolate, blue and gold bands, white shorts
First Season: 1948-49
Nickname: Haven
Records: Attendance: 18,500 v. Wakefield T. (RL Cup) 19 March, 1960
Goals: 141 by J. McKeown, 1956-57
Tries: 29 by W. Smith, 1956-57
Points: 291 by J. McKeown, 1956-57

WIDNES

Ground: Naughton Park
Colours: White jerseys, black shorts

First Season: 1895-96
Nickname: Chemics
Honours: **Division One** Champions, 1977-78
Championship Beaten finalists, 1935-36
Challenge Cup Winners, 1929-30, 1936-37, 1963-64, 1974-75, 1978-79, 1980-81
Beaten finalists, 1933-34, 1949-50, 1975-76, 1976-77, 1981-82
Lancashire League Winners, 1919-20
Lancashire Cup Winners, 1945-46, 1974-75, 1975-76, 1976-77, 1978-79, 1979-80
Beaten finalists, 1928-29, 1939-40, 1955-56, 1971-72, 1981-82
John Player Trophy Winners, 1975-76, 1978-79
Beaten finalists, 1974-75, 1977-78, 1979-80
Premiership Winners, 1979-80
Beaten finalists, 1977-78
BBC2 Floodlit Trophy Winners, 1978-79
Beaten finalists, 1972-73, 1973-74
Western Division Championship Beaten finalists, 1962-63

Records: Attendance: 24,205 v. St Helens (RL Cup) 16 February, 1961
Goals: 140 by M. Burke, 1978-79
Tries: 34 by F. Myler, 1958-59
Points: 316 by M. Burke, 1978-79

WIGAN

Ground: Central Park
Colours: Cherry and white hooped jerseys, white shorts
First Season: 1895-96

Nickname: Riversiders

Honours: **Championship** Winners, 1908-09, 1921-22, 1925-26, 1933-34, 1945-46, 1946-47, 1949-50, 1951-52, 1959-60
Beaten finalists, 1909-10, 1910-11, 1911-12, 1912-13, 1923-24, 1970-71
League Leaders Trophy Winners, 1970-71
Challenge Cup Winners, 1923-24, 1928-29, 1947-48, 1950-51, 1957-58, 1958-59, 1964-65
Beaten finalists, 1910-11, 1919-20, 1943-44, 1945-46, 1960-61, 1962-63, 1965-66, 1969-70
Lancashire League Winners, 1901-02, 1908-09, 1910-11, 1911-12, 1912-13, 1913-14, 1914-15, 1920-21, 1922-23, 1923-24, 1925-26, 1945-46, 1946-47, 1949-50, 1951-52, 1958-59, 1961-62, 1969-70
Lancashire War League Winners, 1940-41
Lancashire Cup Winners, 1905-06, 1908-09, 1909-10, 1912-13, 1922-23, 1928-29, 1938-39, 1946-47, 1947-48, 1948-49, 1949-50, 1950-51, 1951-52, 1966-67, 1971-72, 1973-74
Beaten finalists, 1913-14, 1914-15, 1925-26, 1927-28, 1930-31, 1934-35, 1935-36, 1936-37, 1945-46, 1953-54, 1957-58, 1977-78, 1980-81
BBC2 Floodlit Trophy Winners, 1968-69
Beaten finalists, 1969-70
War League Championship Winners, 1943-44
Beaten finalists, 1940-41

Records: Attendance: 47,747 v. St Helens (League) 27 March, 1959
Goals: 174 by F. Griffiths, 1961-62
Tries: 62 by J. Ring, 1925-26
Points: 372 by F. Griffiths, 1961-62

WORKINGTON TOWN

Ground: Derwent Park

Colours: White jerseys with blue band, white shorts

First Season: 1945-46

Nickname: Town

Honours: **Championship** Winners, 1950-51
Beaten finalists, 1957-58
Challenge Cup Winners, 1951-52
Beaten finalists, 1954-55, 1957-58
Lancashire Cup Winners, 1977-78
Beaten finalists, 1976-77, 1978-79, 1979-80
Western Division Championship Winners, 1962-63

Records: Attendance: 17,741 v. Wigan (RL Cup) 3 March, 1965
Goals: 186 by L. Hopkins, 1981-82
Tries: 49 by J. Lawrenson, 1951-52
Points: 438 by L. Hopkins, 1981-82

YORK

Ground: Wiggington Road

Colours: Amber and black jerseys, black shorts

First Season: 1901-02

Nickname: Wasps

Honours: **Division Two** Champions, 1980-81
Challenge Cup Beaten finalists, 1930-31
Yorkshire Cup Winners, 1922-23, 1933-34, 1936-37
Beaten finalists, 1935-36, 1957-58, 1978-79

Records: Attendance: 14,689 v. Swinton (RL Cup) 10 February, 1934
Goals: 146 by V. Yorke, 1957-58
Tries: 35 by J. Crossley, 1980-81
Points: 301 by V. Yorke, 1957-58

Doug Laughton, now the Widnes coach, with the ball for Widnes against the claret and gold hoops of Huddersfield.

Great Rugby League Players

David Howes

As befits a game founded in 1895, Rugby League has an extensive Hall of Fame. The 13-a-side code has been a showcase for an array of talents ... speed, bravery, handling, kicking, tackling, evasion ... a combination of every sporting skill. The game has provided men of character on and off the field in a sport which is as artistic as it is physical.

CLIVE SULLIVAN, MBE

Clive Sullivan's dream of a rugby career was dogged by a near-fatal timetable of tragedy.

In his early teens, doctors pronounced that he would never be able to walk properly again; his first Rugby League trial resulted in rejection; in only his second Rugby League season, he underwent the first of three serious knee operations; a car accident transported him to death's door; the late 1960s were scarred by three cases of major surgery on both thighs; a footnote was added to the hospital bulletins when operations were performed on his toes.

Yet shortly after 4.30 pm on Saturday, 11 November 1972, Clive Sullivan – having amassed as many stitches as tries – reached out to fulfil a life's ambition.

In the famous Lyons Stadium in France, the Great Britain captain was presented with the Rugby League World Cup. Sullivan had earned himself a place in the annals of outstanding Rugby League players, up there with the fellow Welshman he had idolised since childhood – the inimitable Billy Boston.

Playing in his 20th season in 1982, Sullivan had by then run in more than 300 tries in first-class rugby, including touchdowns in France, New Zealand and Australia. He has played 17 times for Great Britain and 14 for Wales.

His loss of speed after his frequent returns from injury persuaded him to introduce the 'sweeper' role into wing play, continually coming inside to find the ball or the tackle.

His thrilling contribution to Rugby League on the club and international fronts earned him a double major honour. In 1974, Her Majesty the Queen presented the flying wingman with the MBE, while millions of television viewers shared his success story as chronicled on 'This Is Your Life'.

The programme was premature because Sullivan moved from Hull to Hull KR in 1975 and became the first man to score a century of tries for both Humberside clubs. In 1980 he achieved another lifelong ambition by playing for the Robins at Wembley ... against Hull! Ironically, after a season at Oldham, he was to celebrate his 20th year in Rugby League by returning to the Boulevard and playing in the 1982 Cup Final replay at Leeds United F.C. in May, 1982.

ALEX MURPHY

Alex Murphy has written a whole chapter in the illustrious story of Rugby League.

As both player and coach, A. J. Murphy has never been out of the spotlight, and never far away from controversy.

His brilliant talent, both physical and mental, have helped him dominate the Rugby League scene for more than 20 years. Murphy signed for his hometown club St Helens in 1955 and during his stay at Knowsley Road picked up honours for both club and country.

He was a key member of the Saints lineup which captured the League Championship four times in eight years. On the international front, the mercurial halfback won 29 caps with Great Britain and England, touring Australasia twice and starring in the 1960 World Cup.

In 1967, Murphy moved on to Leigh, taking up a new challenge of player-coach. Four years later, his rebuilding plans paid off and Leigh lifted the Challenge Cup at Wembley, shattering the challenge of favourites Leeds.

Murphy had already captained Saints to Challenge Cup success in 1966, and in 1974 Murphy returned with new club Warrington to pick up once again the coveted trophy.

His personal reputation was enhanced in the 1971 Final by his being awarded the Lance Todd Trophy as man-of-the-match.

The highlight of his club coaching career came in 1974 when as player-coach he inspired Warrington to take four major trophies in the same season ... the Challenge Cup, League Leaders Trophy, Player's No 6 Trophy and the Captain Morgan Trophy.

The following year, Murphy returned to the international scene as coach of England in the 1975 World Championship. The tournament spanned Europe and Australasia and England gained second place, being beaten only by Wales in the 'Battle of Brisbane'.

In recent years he was appointed coach of Salford before being taken back to Leigh as manager, lifting the Lancashire Cup and the Championship Trophy in 1981-82, before moving to Wigan as coach in June, 1982.

KEITH FIELDING

After a representative rugby career spanning a decade, Keith Fielding became a world superstar by showing his prowess in events such as rowing, cycling, soccer skills and the obstacle race!

His rise to world fame came in the BBC TV series 'Superstars'. During the 1977-78 season, Fielding was drafted in as a last-minute replacement to battle against sportsmen in events designed to test their all-round capabilities.

The Cheshire physical education master won his British heat convincingly; came second in the European Final; and earned fifth place out of fourteen in the World Final in the Bahamas. He was again British Superstar Champion in 1981.

His achievements grossed him more than £10,000 in prize money, plus round the world travel and international acclaim for both himself and Rugby League.

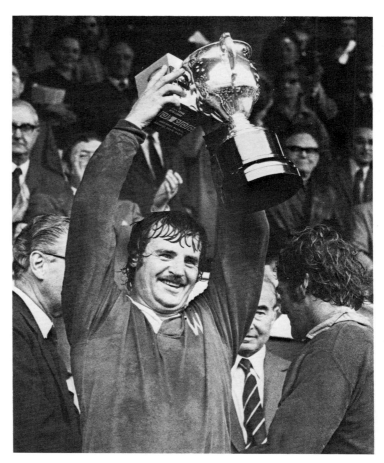

Fielding had already made a name for himself in the field of rugby – in both codes. He received £8,500 from Salford, who invested this substantial amount after seeing the flier touch down nine times in an international Rugby Union seven-a-side tournament at Murrayfield, Scotland.

In his first season, Fielding topped the League try scoring charts with 49 tries, nine ahead of his nearest rival. He made his Rugby League international début within six months of turning professional and marked the occasion at Grenoble, France, with a glorious hat trick.

From that day, the French nicknamed him 'Le Rapide'. He has represented both Great Britain, three times, and England, on seven occasions, in the international Rugby League arena, complementing his 10 England caps in Rugby Union.

NEIL FOX

Neil Fox is the greatest human scoring machine in Rugby League history. His world record total of 6,220 points in a career was amassed between 1956 and

Alex Murphy, prominent in Rugby League for more than one club and in more than one capacity for many years. In 1974, as captain of Warrington, he holds the Rugby League Club Championship Trophy after beating St. Helens.

Clive Sullivan scores in the corner for Hull Kingston Rovers despite the attentions of St. Helens' Peter Glynn. Sullivan has played 20 seasons in Rugby League.

1979. Fox last played first class rugby for Bradford Northern in their opening fixture of 1980, to become one of the elite few to have played top class football at the age of 40.

He was a 16-year-old debutant for Wakefield Trinity at the end of the 1955-56 season and is one of three Fox brothers to have made their mark in Rugby League. Don played with Featherstone Rovers, Wakefield Trinity and Great Britain, Peter was more of a coach, with England, Featherstone Rovers, Bramley and Bradford Northern.

Neil wore Great Britain colours on 30 occasions over a 10-year period, He was a star of the 1962 Great Britain Tour down under, travelling with his brother Don as a team-mate. His biggest disappointment of a distinguished international career was to have to decline the invitation to captain the 1968 World Cup squad because of injury.

His massive points haul features 2,575 goals and 358 tries in 828 appearances. Fox has achieved the rare distinction of scoring 30 or more points in a match on four occasions.

Ironically, Fox had to wait 13 years for the first of his 13 major trophy finals with Trinity, one of the six clubs he has served. The main three were victories at Wembley in the Challenge Cup Final.

Fox will be most remembered for his long service with Wakefield Trinity. Apart from one season at Bradford Northern, he served the Belle Vue club for a 14-year span.

He still holds four club scoring records for Trinity and created a new goalkicking and points record for Hull Kingston Rovers in the 1974-75 season.

In the twilight of his playing career, Fox helped Hull KR and Bramley to promotion to the First Division, and early in 1978 was signed for Bradford Northern, whose coach is brother Peter.

ERIC ASHTON, MBE

A priceless asset for nearly 20 years, Eric Ashton was signed by Wigan for the humble sum of just £250.

Invited to take part in a practice match, Ashton took only 40 minutes to convince the directors that he would be a good buy. This former Scottish Army Rugby Union centre was selected for Lancashire after only seven Rugby League games, his first representative honour in a long chain of success.

St Helens-born Ashton developed into one of the greatest-ever goalkicking centres and captains, for both club and country.

His vast array of achievements, coupled with his diplomacy, earned him the MBE in 1966, the first Rugby League player to receive such an award.

Playing 26 times for Great Britain, he took part in the 1957 and 1960 World Cup tournaments, captaining his side to victory in the latter competition. He also toured Australasia in 1958 and 1962, the second time as captain, when Britain lifted the Ashes.

His international career also included three missionary matches in South Africa in 1957.

On the club front, Ashton's career has been blessed with success. He led Wigan to Wembley on a record six occasions, bringing back the coveted Challenge Cup on three occasions.

In 1963, he took over from Griff Jenkins as player-coach with the Central Park club, graduating to the role of coach in 1969, taking Wigan back to Wembley in 1970. Ashton left his beloved Wigan in 1974 to coach Leeds for a season, before taking the helm at St Helens where the Ashton treatment provided the silverware.

At Knowsley Road, Ashton steered the Saints to two Challenge Cup Finals – 1976 and 1978 – and three consecutive Premiership Trophy appearances, two of them successful. His work with St Helens earned him the inaugural title 'Trumanns Coach of the Year' in a sponsored award scheme in 1977.

He was appointed GB coach for the 1979 Tour of Australasia and took charge of England in 1979 and 1980, announcing his retirement during the 1980-81 season. He returned to St Helens as a director in 1982.

Above *Keith Fielding bursts away for Salford to score a try against Oldham in 1975.*

Left *Keith Fielding.*

Above *Neil Fox,
playing for Bradford
Northern in 1978, near
the end of his career. Fox
holds the Rugby League
total points scoring
record.*

Right *Eric Ashton in
his last Rugby League
role as coach of the Great
Britain side.*

JOHNNY WHITELEY

Johnny Whiteley is a character. One of perfection, fitness, dedication, determination and optimism.

These qualities have earned the stylish loose forward the nickname 'Gentleman John' and justified the respect of colleagues and opponents throughout the ultra-competitive world of Rugby League.

It is those characteristics which Whiteley is now passing on to the stars of tomorrow in his capacity as coach to Great Britain, England and the national Under-24s.

Under his guidance, the Under-24 players have been moulded into a unit which has won all its four matches with the French. Equally important, he has moulded them into players overflowing with his own characteristics which in time will help make them thoroughbred internationals.

Whiteley was born and played in Hull, still speaking with his pronounced West Hull accent. In his early days, his superb loose forward play did the talking ... and silenced fans throughout the North of England and around the world.

He was a key cog in the smooth running Hull side of the 1950s, playing alongside such Rugby League greats as the Drake brothers, Tommy Harris, Mick Scott and Bob Markham.

The took the Boulevard outfit to Challenge Cup and Championship Finals as the black-and-whites, led by Whiteley, thrilled the massive crowds.

Although Whiteley was to earn 14 caps with Great Britain and make two visits down under, his international career was thwarted by a surplus of quality loose forwards, particularly Vince Karalius and Derek Turner. In separate eras, they would each have been first choice number 13s. As it was, the selectors were faced with a headache of the most pleasant type.

When an Achilles tendon injury halted his career in 1968, Whiteley turned to coaching and his perfectionist attitude reached a crescendo two years later when he coached the 1970 Great Britain Tourists to an unbeaten record through Australia and New Zealand.

Having coached the Under-24s since 1976, Whiteley was appointed International Coach for all the national sides in 1980 for a three-year stint, with Colin Hutton as International Manager.

DAVID WATKINS

David Watkins, nicknamed 'The Welsh Wizard', is one of the greatest-ever rugby players to take the field in either code. To prove it, he has excelled in both League and Union, hitting the heights at club and international level.

He made 202 appearances for Newport RU club before switching to the 13-a-side code in October, 1967, for a then record signing-on fee of about £16,000.

He brought with him a massive reputation, with 21 Welsh caps and his country's captaincy. They mattered little as Watkins battled to establish himself in the tough world of Rugby League, where the cynics joked that he could not play because his wallet was too heavy!

The stocky 5ft 6in frame of Watkins had the last laugh. He broke the world goal-kicking record in the 1972-73 season, having already made his international début with Great Britain.

The pinnacle of a player's career – the Great Britain Tour of Australasia – was reached in 1974, only for the dream to become a nightmare when he suffered a broken leg, which put him out of the main part of the visit.

Watkins returned down under a year later as captain of Wales and established himself as the Welsh ambassador for Rugby League, a role which he still fulfils.

He was to go back again in the summer of 1977 in a new and controversial role . . . as coach of Great Britain. Watkins had charge of the Welsh team that year, his side beating arch-rivals England on foreign soil. But his selection as coach to the Great Britain World Championship squad to tour Australasia raised a few eyebrows. Britain lost in the Grand Final to Australia by only one point.

Watkins retired at Salford only to return immediately as a player with Swinton for the 1979-80 season. When Cardiff City decided to enter the League in 1981, they turned to Watkins as Manager of the side, and he took over the coaching role in the autumn when John Mantle was sacked.

STEVE NASH

Scrum-half Steve Nash's reputation as a non-stop player cannot be contested after Great Britain's tour of Australasia in the summer of 1977.

The 5ft 5in number seven played for every minute of every match on the 11-

Above *David Watkins had a long and brilliant career in Rugby Union before joining Salford, and beginning a distinguished spell in Rugby League.*

Left *John Whiteley, who after playing for Great Britain, turned to coaching in 1968, and in 1980 was appointed International Coach for a three-year stint.*

*George Nicholls of
St. Helens swerves to
avoid Colin Dixon of
Salford during the 1976
Premiership Trophy, won
by St. Helens.*

game visit to Australia and New Zealand. In his typical dynamic style, the world-class half-back produced a level of consistency which has kept him on the international scene since his début in 1971.

Nash, weighing in at 11st, was born in the tiny West Yorkshire mining village of Featherstone, a pit community which has unearthed a rich seam of Rugby League talent.

It was a natural progression for the mini-bundle of talent to sign for his hometown club, Featherstone Rovers, putting pen to paper in 1967. During his reign at Post Office Road, Nash was selected for Great Britain and was a key member of the side which captured the World Cup in Lyons in 1972.

On the domestic front, Nash was the mainspring of a strong Featherstone side and his action-packed performance in the Challenge Cup Final of 1973 helped Rovers lift the coveted trophy and gained him the much-prized Lance Todd Trophy, as the adjudged man-of-the-match.

In 1974, Nash packed his bags for the round-the-world trip to Australasia with Great Britain, playing in all six Test matches against Australia and New Zealand. Shortly after his return, he was transferred to big-spending Salford for a then record fee of £15,000.

In his first full season at the Willows, Nash inspired Salford to lift the First Division Championship . . . for the second time in three years. The summer of 1975 saw Nash visiting down under, this time with England's World Championship squad.

Two years later, Great Britain travelled the same route and once again the name Nash was on the roll call, his International tally of caps being 23 for Great Britain and seven for England.

GEORGE NICHOLLS

For seven years, George Nicholls was the cornerstone of British success on the international scene.

As the years have passed, so Nicholls has progressed through the forward positions. His early Great Britain career was shaped

in the loose forward jersey. He moved successfully into the second row and at the start of 1978 launched a new international career at blind side prop.

Whatever position Nicholls occupies, he is the type of forward players want in their own ranks.

His professional career was moulded in 1966 when he signed for his hometown club of Widnes, whom he served for more than six years. While at Naughton Park, Nicholls gained County and International honours, which really piled up after his move to neighbouring St Helens in January, 1973.

The genial packman became a regular choice for Great Britain and England from 1972 and captained England against New Zealand in 1975.

His consistent play has kept him to the forefront in the highly competitive forward battle in Rugby League and his ability as a pack leader is based upon his willingness to set the example.

The selectors chose him to tour down under in 1974, 1975, 1977 and 1979 and on each occasion Nicholls proved to be the perfect tourist.

On the club front, Nicholls ranks among the best forwards in the glittering history of St Helens. For most of his stay at Knowsley Road, he formed a devastating second row partnership with hard-running Eric Chisnall.

Since his conversion to the Saints in 1973, the red and white shirts of St Helens have graced many major finals, including the Challenge Cup Finals of 1976 and 1978.

On the 1979 tour of Australasia Nicholls earned his highest accolade by being named Captain of Great Britain, when Doug Laughton was injured. This was to overshadow even his Lance Todd Trophy award in the 1978 Challenge Cup Final.

After a well-earned Testimonial at St Helens, his career took a new turn when newcomers Cardiff City paid £5,000 for his services and made him captain of the Welsh side for the inaugural 1981-82 season. He moved to Salford for a similar fee in June, 1982.

Steve Nash playing for Salford against Wigan. Nash won the Lance Todd Trophy playing for Featherstone Rovers in 1973.

Rugby Now
Stephen Jones and David Howes

Rugby Union

There is no doubt that rugby union in the 1980s has its frustrations, chiefly because a glittering period in the 1970s has been followed by a period in which the quality of the game has become more mundane. There are also problems relating to the onset of commercialism and professionalism and to teething troubles with new laws. More of these later. However, there is also absolutely no doubt that taking rugby union as a whole the game is in the middle of a boom, an upsurge in interest which is unparalled in almost all other sports. In terms of the countries which participate in rugby, it is now firmly amongst the top four team games in the world and the top six of any type of game. Remarkably, a recent book on the game found around 110 countries in which rugby is played and there were overwhelming suspicions expressed that many more countries see occasional or even regular rugby. The expansion, the rate at which people are discovering the joy of the amateur game, is breathtaking.

Before a more detailed examination of world-wide rugby is made it may be best to discuss the game at home, where, as evidenced in the first chapter, it all started! The basis of top rugby in Britain is the International Championship in which England, Wales, Scotland and Ireland join France annually in the most significant, best supported and usually most dramatic rugby competition in the world. The gladiatorial contests draw thousands to the teeming national grounds at Twickenham, Cardiff, Paris, Edinburgh and Dublin and millions more from all over the world take advantage of live television coverage. Currently, there is a dearth of class players in the Championship, contrasting starkly with the glut of outstanding performers which the mid-1970s threw up. The lack of

class in the Championship is amply illustrated by the fact that all five teams are closely matched and the games are dog fights. In 1981, France were champions and Ireland bottom of the table. In 1982, Ireland were champions and France found themselves at the wrong end. Yet lack of class has not meant lack of excitement and there are still some outstanding players around in British and French rugby, even if the rugby played has been of a rather ordinary, safety-first nature.

England have emerged from a miserable period in their history to contest the last three Championships as sternly as anyone. Despite the enforced retirement of Bill Beaumont, an engaging, formidable and inspiring Lancastrian who pulled England up through sheer effort and personal magnetism, England are proceeding steadily. With experienced forwards like Maurice Colclough and Peter Wheeler and intelligent backs like Paul Dodge and Mike Slemen, their immediate future is bright. They have also ended a long, long period of domination by Wales, who, despite the efforts of their world-class forwards Graham Price and Jeff Squire, have been experiencing lately such a lack of incisiveness in attack and such a lack of playing success relative to their glorious years in the 1970s that the Welsh Rugby Union has set up a committee to enquire into what is going wrong with the game in the country. Nothing is more certain than that Wales will emerge triumphant, sooner or later.

Ireland have always had to choose from distinctly finite resources in their bid to field strong international sides, although the experience and sheer passion of their team, notably of forwards like Moss Keane, Willie Duggan and Fergus Slattery, has often made up for weaknesses elsewhere, and never more so than in Ireland's championship winning side in 1982. Scotland would dearly love to win a Champion-

Moss Keane and a batch of Irish forwards of 1978-79 vintage. Irish forwards have always played with fire, and in 1982 they were rewarded with the Triple Crown.

ship and thereby break a sequence of over 50 years since their last success. Despite the ability of Andy Irvine, their full-back and inspiration for several seasons, and of their clever backs and hard-working forwards, Scotland have still to develop into that formidable side which their current resources might just be able to throw up. A remarkable and attractive win over Wales in the last match of the 1982 season shows what the team can achieve at best.

No team has caused such joy and frustration to their supporters than the fifth member of the Championship, France. The French team has always suffered from inadequate preparation and poor selection. They rarely use the squad training session so esteemed in the other countries to hone their team work, and the predilection of their selectors to make sweeping changes

Mark Ella, one of three Australian brothers to come to the fore in the 1980s, playing against England in 1982 and about to be collared by Mike Slemen and Paul Dodge.

Violence is an increasing problem in modern rugby. Bush of New Zealand attacks Price of the British Lions as he lies on the ground, 1977.

to losing sides rarely allows much in the way of development or continuity. But at their best the French can be a delightful spectacle. They have been led for many seasons by flanker Jean-Pierre Rives, an inspiration and a great man of the game, and have occasionally thrown off their troubles and produced a truly formidable team.

As in France, top European rugby as a whole is in excellent shape despite surface problems. Elsewhere in the world, the picture is much the same, especially in the countries which, with the five Championship nations, make up rugby's governing body, the International Board. These are New Zealand, Australia and South Africa. New Zealand have been fighting hard and often successfully to retain their traditional dominance over Europe although even the All Blacks are hardly overburdened with great players at the moment. The British Lions tour to New Zealand set for 1983 will decide the present balance of power between the Northern and Southern Hemispheres.

Australia's problems in their bid for world rugby union prominence are various. Firstly, rugby union in the country has stiff opposition from rugby league. On the field, the country has never really developed forwards good enough to complement their often brilliant backs. The 1981 Australian tour to the United Kingdom illustrated the class of backs like the remarkable Ella brothers, Glen, Mark and Gary, and of Paul McLean, Roger Gould

and Michael O'Connor. But it also emphasised the problems which Australia have competing in the forwards with the knowledgeable and experienced front five men of the home countries.

South Africa today have problems on the rugby field but these are dwarfed by the problems posed by the onset of politics in sport. For a South African Springboks team to take the field nowadays is an achievement in itself and the 1980 British Lions tour to the country seems like being the last for some time and the final chance for the South Africans to experience top class competition in the foreseeable future.

It is a common but drastic mistake to believe that rugby union begins and ends with the members of the International Board. In fact, the Board directly represents less than one-tenth of the world's rugby players. Everywhere from Andorra to Zimbabwe, from Catholic to Islamic countries, from communist to capitalist countries – in all corners of the world, union is flourishing. Indeed, it is remarkable how the game can cut through religious or political barriers. At the 1982 world sevens in Hong Kong, Argentina played a match against the Barbarians from Britain on the very last day that the Argentinian invasion of the Falkland Islands took place!

The most remarkable strides recently have been made by the communist countries and by America, Canada and Argentina. Russian and Romanian teams are now forces to be reckoned with in the rugby fraternity and the sleeping giants of the game, America and Canada, are now rousing themselves for an assault on the established rugby order.

Indeed, the very expansion which rugby union is undergoing provides the governing body with a problem. How can the International Board give representation to the growing number of non-Board countries while retaining the leadership which has served the game so well for so long. Associate membership for current non-members of the Board may be the answer, with voting rights granted after a suitable period of membership.

It is indisputable that many of the problems which face rugby union today spring from its own success. For example, the many big matches and tournaments are so numerous that pressure on leading players is becoming uncomfortable. This has left the game open to the spectre of professionalism and created many of the same demands on players' time which caused the original schism with the Northern clubs in the last century. Pressure on the top players must be reduced. Violence on the field is a recurring problem but one which merits far less attention than it receives in some sections of the media. The game is certainly no rougher now than in former days and stiffer punishments have helped check some of the misplaced 'enthusiasm' in its tracks.

Problems still arise with the laws and the International Board have not always proved capable enough to alter old laws or create new ones to the good of the game. Too often, laws have proved unworkable or undesirable and there is still something wrong when a handling game like rugby union can be so dominated by the penalty kick at goal. The need to reduce somehow the dependence of teams on their goal-kicker is possibly the most pressing problem in the game.

However, the essence of the game, its essential attractiveness, remains unchanged. Rugby union remains largely true to its ideals, follows the pattern of honest effort on the field and an appealing, thoroughly praiseworthy ability to forgive, forget and enjoy oneself 'après-match'. Rugby union remains unique and largely unspoiled.

Above *France playing England in Paris in 1982. The ball has gone, but the French appear determined not to let Winterbottom reach it.*

Rugby Union is spreading around the world, and outside the home countries, France, New Zealand, Australia and South Africa, one of the strongest countries is Argentina. Sansot with the ball for the Pumas against Southern Counties in 1978.

Rugby League

In the mid-1970s Rugby League was in danger of being kicked into touch.

Morale nose-dived as gates came tumbling down to an all-time low. The structure of the League reverted to two divisions for the third time in the game's history; the limited tackle was fixed at six tackles; other rule amendments were introduced; all this amid a mood of despondency and a general pessimism for the 13-a-side code's future.

In 1974 the new Chairman of the Rugby Football League, Brian Snape, used his high position as a platform for radical change. During the previous decade Mr Snape, owner of a chain of restaurants, cinemas and bingo halls, had injected his expertise into the Salford club and transformed the struggling Manchester outfit into a showpiece operation, complete with new stands and a social complex.

The administration of the game from its Chapeltown Road, Leeds, headquarters, was given a facelift upon the retirement of Bill Fallowfield after nearly three decades of service. His replacement was to be a public school deputy headmaster, David Oxley, who at 35, presented a new dashing image for the Northern game. There followed the introduction of a public relations department as part of a modern marketing approach.

Oxley immediately toured the clubs and the media spreading the gospel according to Brian Snape. It was the heart transplant that was to keep the game alive.

The resurgence of interest and effort in the professional game was being matched by the advancement of the British Amateur Rugby League Association, which had been formed in 1973, plus the formation of a National Coaching Scheme.

It is generally accepted in sport that attendances will not return to the halcyon days of the post-War era. However, from the low ebb of the mid-1970s, Rugby League gates have been on the up-swing. Gates for the First and Second Divisions have risen by 50 per cent in the five years from 1976 to 1981.

The 1980-81 attendances for the League programme totalled 1,647,422 compared with the 1975-76 aggregate of 1,102,421 ... an increase of more than half a million spectators. But the room for further improvement is evident in that the average gate for the First Division is 5,000, and the Second Division 2,000.

The upsurge of Rugby League is also reflected by the commercial progress made in the worlds of television and sponsorship.

Rugby League has been a national television sport since 1951 and is one of the longest-running features of BBC TV's Grandstand marathon. In the 1980-81 season, the intervention of the Office of Fair Trading prevented the BBC from having a monopoly of Rugby League screening and Yorkshire and Granada TV companies introduced a Monday evening edited highlights show, which was to be enlarged for the following campaign, both in the number of matches covered and by the addition of Border TV to the companies showing the programme.

This extensive television exposure was the basis of the development of a sponsorship programme which has brought the Rugby Football League a previously untapped source of revenue. In 1974 only £20,000 was being attracted from business houses. In the 1982-83 season the League's public relations department will be servicing over £325,000-worth of sponsorship contracts.

Every major competition in the game is sponsored and the League's programme of events is further boosted by the clubs' own efforts. At League level, the chief financial backers are State Express, £110,000 for the 1983 Challenge Cup campaign; Slalom Lager, £80,000 for the 1982-83 Championship and Premiership; John Player, £55,000 for their 1983 Trophy tournament; and Dominion Insurance, £40,000

Fulham's first Rugby League game as the first club to carry the league banner in the south for many years. David Allen is caught in possession in the match with Wigan on 14 September 1980.

for sponsoring Great Britain when they tackle the 1982 Australian tourists.

The biggest boost to Rugby League's new image came in the summer of 1980 when Fulham entered the Second Division as the game's first new club since 1954. The birth of a new side based on an existing soccer club in the capital captured the country's imagination and put the 13-a-side code firmly in the national spotlight.

Pioneered by Fulham Chairman Ernie Clay and supported by the likes of Malcolm Macdonald, Colin Welland and former Widnes skipper Reg Bowden, the Fulham initiative was launched in the May, given a champagne send-off at the Rugby League's AGM in June and faced the public with a press call in early September.

For the cost of an average Third Division soccer player, Fulham's £200,000 investment into Rugby League brought them a side which attracted nearly 10,000 people to Craven Cottage to see the South's only Rugby League side hammer Wigan 24-5 on their début. Fulham continued to hog the headlines winning 20 of their 28 matches to gain promotion at the first attempt.

This concept of sharing ground facilities, coupled with the low cost of promoting Rugby League compared with soccer, attracted the attention of other football clubs. The Fulham experiment proved that a stadium could house the 11- and 13-a-side games with the minimum of problems and the maximum of benefits to be gained for duplicated sales of tickets, programmes,

Roy Holdstock of Hull Kingston Rovers playing for Great Britain against New Zealand in 1981.

advertising, souvenirs etc.

Inquiries from other soccer clubs passed double figures and overdraft-conscious directors studied the profit-making potential of staging Rugby League in stadia for which expenses were all being paid. As Fulham headed for the top of the Second Division table, the Rugby League authorities encouraged Carlisle United and Cardiff City to apply for League membership.

Carlisle were admitted at the March 1981 meeting and the Welshmen a month later, bringing the total of professional clubs to 33, the highest since the turn of the

Cardiff Rugby League team after their formation for the 1981-82 season. Back: M. Nicholas, P. Ringer, A. Karalius, A. Bailey, J. Mantle (coach), C. Seldon, A. Daley, P. Rowe, T. David, D. Jenkins. Middle: K. Gwilliam, G. Pritchard, P. Woods, G. Nicholls, S. Fenwick, M. Marshall, D. Jones. Front: R. Fleay, C. O'Brien, G. France, A. Garritty.

century. Sixteen clubs contest the Slalom Lager Championship and the remaining 17 battle it out in the Second Division, the League operating on a four-up, four-down basis.

This ground-sharing with soccer principle is likely to develop further although the advent of a trio of new clubs inside 15 months brought about fears of a drain on top-flight talent. This has been countered by a belief that clubs should spread their scouting nets and already Fulham have signed a threequarter all the way from Morocco!

Rugby League has also extended its boundaries on the International front with the acceptance of Papua New Guinea as members of the International Board, joining traditional members Britain, Australia, New Zealand and France. The British League has also invested about £60,000 in an attempt to launch the game in America, while new drives are being made to start Rugby League in Italy.

Great Britain has been second best in the International arena since 1972 and the powers-that-be have made the revitalisation of the national side a priority, beginning with the visit of the Australian Tourists in the autumn of 1982, highlighted by a three-match Test series.

Rugby League has been notorious for changing the rules of the game, to such an extent that each country had a large number of local laws and one set which were applied for International matches. When this reached an almost farcical level it was decided at the 1980 International

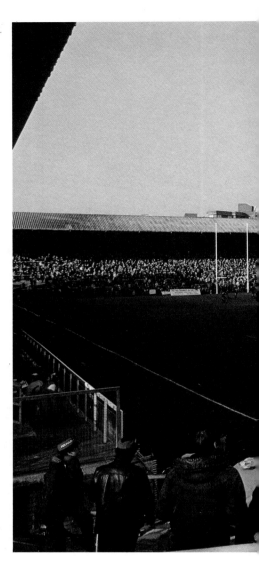

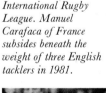

International Rugby League. Manuel Carafaca of France subsides beneath the weight of three English tacklers in 1981.

Board meeting that one set of International rules would be confirmed for use by each individual country and this unilaterally accepted rule book was introduced into Britain at the start of the 1981-82 season.

As Rugby League progresses through the 1980s as one of Britain's few growth sports, the authorities have been careful to monitor the image of the game. The smaller crowds have not made Rugby League as attractive as soccer for the hooligan and the small pockets of trouble have been quelled by the clubs' keenness for prosecution and the adverse reaction of the genuine fan.

More and more money is being sidelined for ground improvements as Rugby League bids to live up to its slogan as being 'The man's game for all the family'.

Above *The Fulham Football Club ground at Craven Cottage, once the home of Johnny Haynes, and now the Sunday home of Rugby League.*

Rugby League under-11s putting on a show before the Rugby League Cup Final. These matches are an enjoyable preliminary to the big match each year.